A Special Pilgrim's Progress

Mary Francess Froese

YorkshirePublishing
www.yorkshirepublishing.com
Write Now.

Yorkshire Publishing
3207 South Norwood Avenue
Tulsa, Oklahoma 74135
www.YorkshirePublishing.com
918.394.2665

This book is dedicated to
Shirley Boyer, Joel's friend
And the one who said this story
should be written.
I love you

"Behold, I send an angel before You to keep you in the way and Bring you into the place which I Have prepared."

Exodus 23:20

This is not a religious book, but rather a book about a partnership. It is between a devastated young couple and the One who can turn the greatest tragedy in one's life into a channel of blessing that touches everyone. Not to tell the story would be a travesty because that help and hope is for everyone who has a need and reaches out to the One in that need.

The book has been in the making for fifty-six years and can only now be told because there is now an ending to the story.

If you aren't a reader and come to this book,

I would urge you to, at least, read the epilogue, at the end. It is a WOW! Thanks to "The One!"

Your Baby Is A Vegetable!

Joel Allen Froese was our first child. Born May 27, 1960, when I was nineteen and Allen was twenty-four. By this time we'd been married two years. In Oklahoma City in the 60's to make it a year without having a baby was a rare thing. Allen and I were so in love. The first year of our marriage we determined we wouldn't have a television, but would spend the time learning about each other. Of course, when you are young and so in love that meant lots of "naps!" These naps also added to the wonder that there was no baby on our first anniversary. I will, however, admit to being a little nauseous when we went to the famous Cattlemen's Restaurant to celebrate this first milestone. And shortly thereafter the first little episodes of nausea became gut wrenching dates with the toilet bowl. I had never been so sick in my life. When I made an appointment to see a doctor I was afraid that I had some terminal disease. When the doctor told us we were pregnant, as thrilled as we were, it was hard to celebrate...Ugh!

Our baby was the most beautiful thing we'd ever seen. A perfectly normal seven and one-half pound brown-eyed miracle. We were the first in our gang to have a baby and were determined that we wouldn't allow him to slow down our fast lifestyle. Joey, the nickname we had

1

chosen for him, went to poker when he was a week old and out to dinner that same week. My mom said, "You'all need to be careful. He is just a little baby. He could be more susceptible to germs."

One evening we had friends visiting us when Joel began to throw up. Upon checking his temperature, we found he had enough of a fever to let Dr. Schnitz, his pediatrician, know. He sent out some medication and said, "Don't worry if Joel sleeps longer than usual…these suppositories will take care of the problem." So, we allowed him to sleep throughout the night and into the next day. When Joey continued to sleep into the afternoon, my husband, Allen, finally said, "I'm going to try to wake him. He needs to eat something." Allen went to the nursery and did everything possible to awaken him, with no success. He was non-responsive. Hearts pounding, we quickly phoned Dr. Schnitz and he told us to meet him at his office. With our babe wrapped in Allen's arms, our steps echoed through the empty halls on this Sunday afternoon. After taking one look, Dr. Schnitz said, "Let's get him over to the hospital."

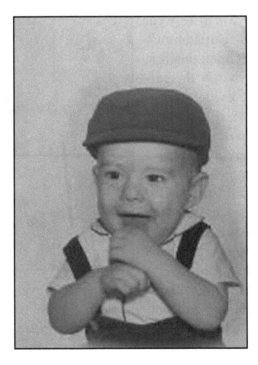

By the time we'd checked him in, we began to pray. We'd had no time for God in these young days of our marriage but now it was time for an SOS to Heaven. An hour later Joel began to have convulsions. With no let up in sight, the Doctor strapped his arm to a board so that the IV couldn't be jerked out of his arm. Eight long days passed. They tested his toys for poison....checked his formula for poison....did a spinal tap. Still in a coma after six days of convulsions, the doctors had come up empty. By day eight, Joey had come out of the coma and was so pumped full of anti-convulsion medications there was some minutes when he was seizure free. But there was still no diagnosis. All the physicians who had been consulting with our Pediatrician had only one catch all disease, meningitis. Sadly, Joey was placed into Allen's arms and what we were told made shivers of dread course down my back, "Your little son is a vegetable. You need to put him away and forget about him! ...oh, yes, and by the way. You can never take him around people. With the sulfur drugs he is on, the slightest infection would kill him!"

We walked out of that hospital in helpless shock. Those were the days before baby car seats so when we get to the car Allen handed Joel to me in the front seat and I tenderly cocooned him to my breast as we made our way home, as silent tears coursed down my cheeks. In those eight days in the hospital... an eternity, our little boy had reverted to infancy. He couldn't even hold his head up.

After arriving home, Allen gently laid Joel in his baby bed and he took me by the scruff of my neck and propelled me to our bedroom. As we got to the bed he pushed me down to my knees and he got down beside me. Our tears began to mingle together as we cried out to God for His help. As I have looked back over our lives, I am confident that when we sent that prayer heavenward, our God said to those in attendance to that prayer,

"You see that young couple down there. They have asked Me for My help in their great despair.

I'm going to take this great tragedy from our enemy and I'm going to turn it so that it becomes the greatest blessing in their lives."

No More Doctors

In the ensuing days, we took Joey to the doctor's office daily for an injection of ACTH for his seizures. Finally, the day came when Dr. Schnitz said to us, "You all are going to have to begin giving Joey his injections. This isn't practical or cost effective for you to keep bringing him to the office. So, we began to practice giving injections on an orange. What a trip! Allen could look at a needle and pass out! I was so squeamish I grumbled, "If I'd have thought I could give someone a shot, I'd have become a nurse! I CAN'T DO THIS!!!" But it had to be one of us. The day came and I held the needle in my hand. I looked at Allen and he looked at me. Sweat pouring off both our faces. Joey looked up at us in his sweet innocence and I plunged the needle in his leg and promptly blacked out. Allen grabbed me and the needle. He propped me up with his own leg while he completed giving the shot, then lowered me to the ground. He was the chosen one! Every day for years, he would give Joey his injection before he left for work in the mornings. During the daytime when he was off at work and Joey would quit breathing, I'd be the one to call the fire department. They were wonderful and were there in a flash with their pull motor.

My parents were as frantic as we were about the diagnosis that Joey was a vegetable. We were all grasping at straws for an answer. When my mother called me and said, "Why not try chiropractic to see if that would help?" We jumped onto the idea! Every day Allen would get off work early and we'd bundle Joey up for a ride across Oklahoma City to the chiropractor. We did this daily for several months but when we saw no improvement and our money ran out we reluctantly stopped the treatments. (Years later, when Joel was a teenager, he was with me when I went into the chiropractor to receive a treatment. I introduced him to Joel and he said, "Have you ever tried chiropractic for him?" I told him of our experience when he was a baby and he replied, "That is why your son is not totally spastic and in a wheel chair today! You kept the cerebral fluid running during those early days.!" Praise God!)

Life limped along. We were almost prisoners in our own home.... no one could come into the house nor could we take Joel out among people. We bought a new stereo system and allowed that to be our interaction with the world. We tried to live as sterile a life as we could.

The biggest struggle in our lives now, was the inability to get Joey to eat. Allen would prop him up in his infant seat and hold his head while trying to get a few spoonsful of food down him. Joey would writhe back and forth, waving his hands in front of his face making it very difficult to get him still long enough to aim the spoon at his mouth. Finally, in desperation, we put a big hole in the nipple of his bottle and fed him baby food that way. He could no longer even hold his bottle. He couldn't turn over, nor sit up unaided. I would try to prop him up with pillows but his body was getting heavier and before I knew it, he was on his face.

Throughout all these difficulties, Allen and I continued to grow in our love and dependence for one other. And, as young couples do, we adjusted to our lives and were happy. Together, we watched Gunsmoke, Andy Griffith and the Carol Burnett Show. One night I came into the kitchen where Allen had just taken a cherry pie out of the oven. He had carved "I love you" into the top of the pie. The cherries had oozed out over the crust and I was so touched I took a photo of it. I truly felt loved by this man.

An appointment was made with the Department Head of Child Neurology at the University of Oklahoma to give us his opinion. During the visit, we lay Joey on a pallet on the floor and he observed him. For fifteen minutes he sat silently watching our dear little son. Then he shook his head and said to me, "Little Mama, your baby is a vegetable!"

How in the world could anyone watch a baby lying on the floor for fifteen minutes and give such a diagnosis? I was so angry, I picked up my baby and stormed out of his office, weeping. I declared to myself, "That's it! No more doctors. We'll just deal with what comes ourselves!

(Four years later, I saw this doctor at the Oklahoma City Zoo. I walked over to him, holding Joey's hand as he toddled beside me and I said hello. I made sure he saw that the little boy who stood beside me was the so-called vegetable.)

Terrified

Yes, terrified! That was the first feeling I had when I discovered I was pregnant again. My first thought - will this baby be normal? For the whole nine months I ran the gamut of emotions from terrified to euphoric. I was so emotional and scared. I wanted this baby in the worse way but my imagination just ran wild thinking of all the things this new baby could have wrong with him.

Six months into the pregnancy, we heard that some of our friends had their house up for sale and just wanted someone to take over the payments. We jumped at the chance to be homeowners. We moved into our new home with great joy, taking this as a sign that everything would be okay and we prepared for our new baby.

Joey was almost two years old and could barely sit alone, much less walk. He was really a heavy load to carry around, nine months pregnant, so I began to have lots of pressure in my abdomen. My sweet husband did everything he could to help me. I craved ice, so he would stand at the sink and crush ice for me until his hands froze. (His gift to me after having the baby was an ice crusher…but by then the craving was gone!) Disposable diapers were unheard of in the 60's, so Allen hung up cloth diapers in the freezing cold. In Oklahoma, as soon as the wet clothes hit the clothesline they froze. When you saw them flapping in the breeze you knew they were dry. By now Joey was wearing two diapers at a time.

We were a young couple who longed for "normal." Scott Andrew was born April 12, 1962. He was normal in every way. We brought him home and placed him in the beautiful bassinet that my mother made for him. For just a couple of weeks we kept him in the room with us at night because we were concerned how he would adjust to Joel's nightly crying. It was just something we all had to deal with. It took Joey about two hours each night to cry himself to sleep. It still breaks my heart when I think why we couldn't get to the bottom of his crying. However, when we moved Scott into the room with Joey they both adjusted and he could sleep through anything.

Carrying around two babies really took its toll on my back. I was young – only twenty-two; but my back would go into spasm and the pain was so excruciating I couldn't get out of bed some days. In one terrible episode, I didn't know what in the world I was going to do. Allen insisted he had to go to work. He was so conscientious about his job…never missing a day for anything! He fed my babies breakfast and placed them in the floor in the bedroom where I lay. Thankfully, both boys were content for the moment, but now Allen was gone and I was alone. He had called our next door neighbor who graciously said she would check in on us in an hour or so. When she came over we called my mother. She said she didn't have a car, but if I could get the kids to her she would watch them for the day. I called a taxi and told the dispatcher my dilemma. When the taxi arrived, that driver came into the house with great purpose; picked up my boys and took them to my mother.

Finally, hours later, I was resting comfortably when the front doorbell rang. It took all my strength to pull myself up out of bed and shuffle to the door. Standing at the front door with a big smile was a florist delivery man. He held a beautiful floral arrangement in his hands. Allen had sent me flowers! If he'd have been there right then, I'd have poured them over his head! I was so mad.

This work thing never went away. I had to do some horrendous things by myself because Allen wouldn't take time off work. But how do you fault a man so driven to provide for his family?

If You Were To Die Today!

Standing at my sink, one day, doing dishes, I began to count my blessings. I had a lovely new home; new furniture; and an automatic washing machine; two beautiful babies, a husband who loved me. Yet, I thought, *why am I so lonely???* This thought had been popping into my head regularly. A few days prior, Allen and I had been on a very rare night out with our friends. We were out dancing and drinking. I watched them all having fun and I sat there overcome with loneliness. Where on earth was this coming from? This thought continued to plague me throughout the summer.

On a hot Oklahoma summer day, I was cleaning my house as I did every day, sweat dripping from my body. I heard a knock at the door. Opening the door, I wiped my face and smiled, saying, "Hello." A middle aged woman stood at the door and said,

"Hi, I'm taking a church survey. May I ask you a couple of questions?"

"Sure," I replied.

"If you were to die today, do you know where you'd spend eternity?"

I was jarred by the question but I managed to reply, "Yes, and I'm not at all happy about it!"

The woman said, "Thank you for your time!" and she was gone.

I just stood there with my mouth open. In the following days, her question resonated in my mind and my spirit… *If you were to die today, do you know where you'd spend eternity?* I was still puzzled as I told Allen about this strange encounter at our front door.

A few weeks later a Bible salesman came to the door and I bought his biggest Bible, placing it on the coffee table. Okay! Now I reckoned that was a step in the right direction.

The first election in which I was old enough to vote came in early November, 1962. I proudly voted for John Kennedy. Was there ever such a popular young president. My parents had never ever paid attention to the election process in our country. We never flew the American flag. I had not been taught anything patriotic (that was one of the reasons I thought I must be adopted) I loved being an American. Everything lacking in my growing up family life I WANTED in my own family. I knew this to be very important! I registered to vote on the last day of registration…the day I got out of the hospital from having Scott. I sorely waddled to the place of registration but I was determined. Finally, I had reached the age where I could vote…and vote I did! I was over the moon! I had actually cast my first ballot. So here I was at twenty-two years old; the mother of two sons, one husband and a citizen in good standing. Could there possibly be more??? ***If you were to die today do you know where you'd spend eternity???*** This question was still resonating in my spirit.

Within a few days of the election, Allen came down with a bad case of quiet. Day after day this already silent man would come home from work and say n o t h i n g! Finally, one night in desperation, I fed the babies early, placed them in their room with their toys and made a nice dinner for just the two of us. He came through the door; took off his coat and sat down at the table. I sat across from him, trying to smile reassuringly. We sat in silence for a long period of time until he held out his hand to me and said, "Take my hand baby, we're going to pray!"

"What???" I said, in shock and surprise.

He looked at me and smiled; "Today, in the bathroom at work I gave my heart to Christ. God told me it was now or never! I just want you to know, I've quit drinkin', smokin', and cussin'." I was so thrilled, I ran around and jumped into his arms. We talked, we laughed, we cried. We poured the contents of all our fancy liquor bottles down the drain and pitched out the bottles. My husband laughed, "I told the guys at work I'd bum cigarettes as long as they'd let me." All those days he had been so silent he'd been under the conviction of his sin…and now he was free!

That Saturday evening when our friends came over to play cards, they looked at Allen with curiosity. Allen, usually while playing cards would normally let off a string of expletives. This night – nothing! After the card game there were no cocktails...only cokes. We never let on what had happened to us and they all left our home shaking their heads.

The next morning we hired a neighbor girl to watch the boys while we went to find a church. We had no idea what type of church we wanted to attend. I had attended a Pentecostal church growing up. Every time I'd take a friend to church with me, someone would shout or dance or speak in a strange language and embarrass me to death so I knew I didn't want any part of that. Allen had been reared in a Mennonite church and felt much the same as I. So, on this momentous day, we determined we would start driving and we would stop at the first church we came to as long as it wasn't Pentecostal or Mennonite. In Oklahoma City there was a Baptist church on every corner, so we pulled up in front of Classen Blvd. Baptist Church.

We hadn't been inside a church in several years and had no idea what to expect. While we were dating we both said we wanted a "Christian home" but we'd been young and having fun and hadn't gotten there yet.

Now, here we were. When the music started - every song was designed for us. Every word the preacher spoke zeroed in to our hearts. We sat and cried all throughout the whole hour. At the end of the service we knew we should respond in some way but we didn't know how they did it in a Baptist church so we just sat there. It didn't take long for the preacher to make his way toward us. He motioned for us to follow him. He took us into his office and we told him what had happened in our lives. We cried for what seemed like hours. It was the most healing, cleansing time of my life with my husband sharing in every moment.

Bro. T.P. Haskens was the interim pastor in this church and he instantly became our Apostle Paul. We loved that man who made Jesus real in our hearts and lives. From that moment, November, 1962, we never looked back on our old lives. We became members of that little Baptist Church the next Sunday and as we stood in line so the church family could greet us, there was the woman who had come to my door that summer day, with her stinging question (If you were to die today do you know where you'd spend eternity). Now she smiled knowingly as she shook our hands to welcome us into the family of God.

Our New Lives

Allen and I were baptized the last Sunday of November, 1962. We immediately committed to tithing, gladly giving to God the first ten percent of our income. However, the very next month Allen came home with a very troubled look on his face. Oh dear! I thought. "What's wrong honey?"

Allen replied with a frown, "It's almost pay day, and I realized that after we pay our tithe, and take care of our bills, there will be no money for Christmas."

"Oh!" I replied shakily.

Then it immediately came to me what to respond to him. "Honey, we're committed to the tithe. We have seen it in God's Word. The kids will be okay. They are so little. (Scott was six months old and Joel was two and a half.) It's our new life as Christ followers. We're just going to have to trust that God will do what's best for us!" Allen nodded with relief.

A couple of days later he came in waving a letter. "Look, it's a letter from our escrow account. They say we've overpaid our escrow account and we don't owe a rent payment this month!"

"Look what the Lord has done!" We danced around the kitchen with great joy.

Indeed! Look what the Lord hath done! The amazing thing was that as we asked our neighbors if they had a similar thing happen to them, each said no. This was our first miracle!!! This was the singular event that we would always look back to, all throughout our lives when our financial situation would become tough and we were tempted to use the money rather than trust the Lord.

One day I was standing at the sink, doing dishes when it occurred to me...***I'm not lonely! I feel so happy and content! Jesus has taken my loneliness and filled me with Himself!***

A month or so after we were baptized, we realized we couldn't continue to hire a babysitter in order to go to church. This was the first time we really prayed together as a couple,

"Father, we can no longer afford a babysitter and, besides, we want to take our babies to church with us. You know the doctors have told us the slightest infection would be fatal to Joel, so Father God, we give him to You. We are asking that You would keep Joel safe from all infection."

With our prayers lifted up to God for Joel's safety, every Sunday morning and evening and Wednesday nights we would bundle our babies up and we'd all go to church. Our new life had officially begun. Our boys were so happy to be in the church nursery with all the other little ones. Those dear women attending to the children were so loving with all the kids. And Joey took his first steps in the church nursery.

So Long Bottles!

Our new Christian home and family had become very rewarding to Allen and me, except there was just one more thing we needed to do. The boys were both on a bottle way too long. I thought it was unfair for Scotty to have to give up his bottle while Joey was still so dependent on his. One day, my husband – always thinking – said we were going for a ride. He gave both the boys their bottles when we got into the car.

About midway in the drive Allen said, "Scotty, give me your bottle." Scotty handed it over to his daddy who promptly threw it out the window. The boys and I were shocked! My dear husband hadn't clued me in as to what he was going to do. He then said, "Joey, give me your bottle!" and Joey reluctantly handed it over. His daddy promptly threw his bottle out the window also. (We normally would never litter!) A wail came from the back seat. Both boys were now crying.

Allen pulled the car over to the curb and turned to face them. Tenderly he said, "Boys, you are too big for those old bottles. You will do just fine without them. I love you, okay?"

Oh, boy! more work for mom! But I was very thankful that my husband was strong enough to do this difficult thing. It had to be done not just for the boys - but for their mother, as well. Whatever Scotty did, Joey tried to emulate and within a couple of days they were drinking from cups like pros and the bottles were a distant memory.

Uh Oh!

The next year after we'd given our hearts to Jesus, Allen was "set aside" as a deacon candidate, by the church deacon board. We had been such good students and had learned the Bible rapidly. Our whole lives revolved around that little Baptist Church in Oklahoma City, so it seemed the logical next step…except for one blip. We were young and in love and the polaroid camera had just been developed! Allen brought one home from the office and one evening we had fun as he posed me for nude photos. We felt a little naughty… so Allen locked them in his stash closet.

After Sunday evening service the next week, we came home from church and were putting the boys to bed when I noticed little red drips of wax coming down a wall under a window near one of the baby beds. I called Allen, "Honey, come look here!" He came in and we began following this trail of red wax with a flash light. The drips were so tiny it has hard to see them. The trail went first to his clothes closet. He scanned the shelf where he unloaded his trousers after work. Our hearts sank, his watch was gone!

We then saw that the trail continued to lead us to his stash closet. As he unlocked it, the door came off in his hands. The screws from the hinges were gone. The first thing he dug for were those nude photos. We breathed a huge sigh of relief when we found them. It appeared that nothing was missing…maybe the thieves was scared off as they heard our car pull into the garage and they had to flee.

Allen took those photos and straightaway cut them into a million pieces and flushed them down the toilet. We didn't know how far the deacon board might go to investigate a candidate… we later laughed about how ridiculous it was to think that a bunch of church people would break into a house to check out whether someone was "deacon" material.

We later found out some of the neighbor boys was breaking into houses.

Options

My husband and I continued to deal with Joel's grand mal seizures, which were only partially controlled by the daily injections of ACTH. I became a member of a support group for parents of retarded children. (This was the term used for kids like Joey during those years.) In listening to all the different stories, I came to realize that for whatever reason, the statement the doctors had shocked us with was common. "Your child is a vegetable…you need to put him away and forget him!" Maybe it was meant to serve as a lightning rod to awaken us to the seriousness of our new life. Perhaps if we became angry, it would give Allen and me the courage we needed to fight for our special child. This devastating statement from the doctors, for whatever reason it was said to us, it served to reveal to us our resolve to do whatever we could for Joel.

When Joey was about four, we left him with dear friend, Marilee Todd, for a day while Allen and I visited a state facility for the mentally handicapped. We were shown into a huge room where children from about one year to five years old were crawling around on the floor. The room was hot enough that they were comfortable in only a diaper, with no other clothes on. There was absolutely no furniture in that room. And precious few toys scattered around. A TV was mounted WAY up on a wall where little children crawling around on the ground could not benefit from it even if it showed all the kiddy shows of the day. Attendants stood around the walls. They didn't even have chairs to sit in. I wanted to scream when I saw this. Next, they showed us the older children. Most were confined to beds – in the middle of the day. It was horrible!!! These children held out their hands toward us…needing a touch from somebody, anybody! I was almost hysterical when we left there. NO WAY!!! NO WAY!!! Would my child ever be exposed to this!!!

When we returned to the Todd's home to pick up the boys I was still a basket case. As I walked into the house, I just fell into Marilee's arms, weeping. She didn't look like she'd had such an easy day of it either. Thankfully, her daughter, thirteen-year old Amy, had a heart for Joey. She didn't care if he dragged out all the toys into the playroom and had magazines strewn all over the floor.

This family truly became our dearest friends. They discipled us all as a family as we grew in our new faith.

John and Marilee Todd were about ten years older than Allen and I and they had a daughter, Elaine, who was Scott's age. Amy was about thirteen and Stephen was in high school. They had really reached out to us as new Christians and we so appreciated them. We were told that John was a "sanitarian." I thought that was a nice word for garbage man. I also thought the city of Oklahoma City must pay their garbage-men well, as Marilee wore a mink stole to church.

One evening we had a very formal dinner at church and John came in his "uniform." Allen and I looked at each other, as we sat across from them at the table. It was a navy-blue, double-breasted suit with all sorts of hash marks at his heart. When introductions were made from the dais, John was introduced as Admiral Dr. John G. Todd, of the United States Public Health Corps. I almost slid under the table! We would never have felt comfortable with this family if we'd known that! But they already loved us and we already loved them... We have laughed about that a million times through the years. John later became the Under Secretary to the Surgeon General, Everett Koop.

Soon after our visit to the state home for the mentally retarded, a friend showed us an article about a new technique to help retarded children. It was called "patterning." Either Allen or I would have to go to Dallas to learn the procedure. It involved having a team of four people, one at each limb of the child. All would work in sync to simulate the crawling motion. For a set amount of time every four hours, this technique was repeated; which would mean having at least twelve people coming in and out of our house every day of the week. Everything in the household would surround this four-times-daily event. Since it was so new and controversial, I spoke with my pediatrician about it. We talked in depth about the logistics of finding twelve people who would commit twenty minutes each day to travel to our home to be a part of the team. The whole idea just made my head swim. How on earth could that be maintained? It was a seven day a week commitment. After much thought and prayer Allen and I decided against this. I've always prayed we did the right thing. (All throughout the years I've never heard anyone say they or their child had been helped by this technique).

After the boys began to walk and their boundaries expanded, they weren't always within arms' reach to rescue if needed, so Allen devised an action that I thought amazing. He would snap his finger and whatever the boys were doing they would stop and look at daddy. This idea was a God-send for us. If either of the boys were close to danger; if they got close to a roadway; if they walked too far away from us; they would hear that snap and immediately they would stop and look at their daddy. I never saw either of my boys defy this precious snap. When

Joey began to walk, his gate was like a trot. I'd have to run to catch him. Not dad! That one snap would get his attention and he would immediately stop and look back at dad. (When Joel was grown and home for a visit, Allen tried that technique and Joel immediately waved his hand at dad and said "NO!")

Our Boys

Those were such happy days for our little family. Joey and Scott were inseparable. When Scott came along it was like a lightbulb went off in Joey. He could see what he was supposed to be doing. He would try to imitate Scott as he crawled about the house. The best Joey could do was pull himself on his arms, not being able to get his legs under him to crawl. But he was never far behind his brother. After Scott learned to sit alone, it wasn't long before Joey was able to push himself up into a sitting position. By this time Joey was almost three.

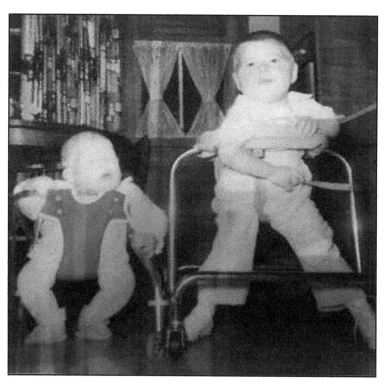

When we bought our Bibles, Joey was captivated by them. We, of course, carried our Bibles to church and we'd read them at home. However, we couldn't leave those Bibles anywhere or Joey would grab them. One day I walked in on him sitting on the floor with my Bible in his hands. He was going through it, page by page. He drooled and every page was sopping wet. I came up behind him and said, "NO!" and retrieved the Bible. He began to scream…. bloody murder! And, he didn't stop until I handed it back to him. Obviously, the Bible was ruined for me, but it was his prize possession. It also didn't last but a few days for him. When I had to take it from him to throw it away, there were only a few scattered pages left, but he was broken hearted. I began to scour the Good Will or the Salvation Army thrift stores for cheap copies that I could have on hand for him. He never tired of them. He would sit for hours paging through the Bibles. Grandma and grandpa and aunts and uncles would watch him in wonder. We all wondered what was going on in his mind?

When it was time to get Scotty a walker to help him learn to walk, we scoured catalogues and found a larger version for Joey. For weeks they both followed me everywhere banging up my walls. They were so happy with this mode of travel. However, after a few months of this I began to be a little concerned when Scotty wasn't venturing out to walk on his own.

He was about fourteen months old and was content to crawl wherever he needed to go or toddle around in the walker. I guess since Joey didn't walk he didn't see the logic. To encourage him, I began to stand Scotty up along a wall and we'd sing Sunday School songs and I would hold out my hands for him to walk to me. Joey wasn't having any part of that. He wanted to stand upright himself. So I stood them both side-by-side. Scotty caught on pretty fast to reach out for my hands, taking steps. After a couple of days of Scotty practicing, I looked over at Joey. He was ready! My heart lurched within me! "Come on Joey, reach my hand!" Until now, he hadn't been able to stand alone. Now, with his one hand crammed into his mouth for support, he held out his other hand and wobbled toward me. He was almost four years old and very shaky on his feet. I was amazed when he took two steps….and then three. I grabbed both boys, weeping and laughing, and we rolled around on the floor. God is soo good!

Cleaning and rearranging my house was my hobby, when I wasn't attending to my boys, so I was happily working about one morning, listening to my Christian radio station and I realized I hadn't seen the boys in a while. I got down on my knees and began to crawl about the house to see why things were so quiet. Hearing lots of giggling on the other side of their bedroom door I slowly opened it. Scott was slathering Vaseline all over Joey's head and face. His eyes were glued shut and his hair was standing on end. I yelled, "Boo!" They both about jumped out of their skin....Their first sneaky, getting caught, episode. We again rolled around on the floor, laughing. It took me an hour to get the goo off them and the walls. A few weeks later, on a hot, sweaty Oklahoma summer day, I'd stripped the boys of all clothing but their diapers and placed them on the clean cement garage floor where it was cool. There were toys there for them to play with. After awhile I looked out to see what they were up to and I was dumbfounded!

Where in the world had they gotten chocolate chips? There they sat in their diapers, surrounded by chocolate chips, melted chocolate smeared all over them, busily cramming more in their mouths. What a mess! I plopped them both in the kitchen sink and scrubbed the chocolate off them, redressed and stuck them in their beds and then tackled the garage floor to clean up the chocolate mess of fun.

One evening, hearing giggling from the kitchen, I wandered in to see Allen place first one boy and then the other, atop the refrigerator. "Come on, jump....I'll catch you." Squealing, they would each propel themselves off the frig and into dad's arms. "Allen, what in the world are you doing? They might get hurt!"Nah, I won't drop them....I'm teaching them to trust me!" Oh, my gosh, how can such a little exercise claim such huge results. My boys learned to trust their daddy. In the months and years to follow this trust was played out over and over.... And all because of a simple exercise with tiny little boys.

In the evenings at our house, after the boys were in the pajamas their grandmother lovingly made for them, we would go into the living room and we would sit on the couch and I would take the large family Bible onto my lap and I would read them the stories of David and Goliath, Sampson, Noah and the Ark. They loved to see the large color pictures that went with the stories.

Then we would go into their bedroom and we'd all get on our knees and talk to Jesus.

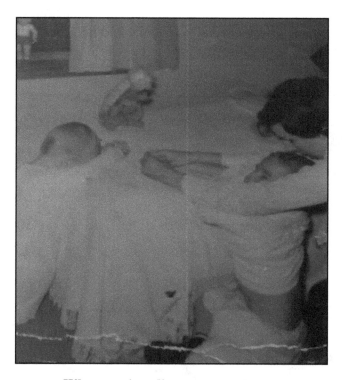

What precious lives entrusted to us

In order to get away a bit, I began putting Joey in a Mother's Day Out one morning a week. A church in Oklahoma City had begun this as a ministry to the community and what a wonderful thing it was. I remember so vividly one little girl. She was about four years old and had no limbs. She was just a torso. She was the cutest little thing with a long, blond pony tail. Her mom and older brothers would bring her in to play and she would giggle and squeal as they tossed her about like a football. We, who observed the way her family loved and interacted with her, were rather taken aback by the cavalier way her brothers treated her disability, but it was a lesson, as well. She was happy and the center of attention in a big loving family. I was so proud that I could finally take Joey out of the car and place him on the ground, take his hand and walk him into the church, with that left hand forever stuck into his mouth. That seemed to be his stabilizer, giving him the security he needed. He drooled terribly and my mother had begun to make him big boy bibs. He always had a huge smile and his front teeth, decayed from all the seizure medication, had to be overlooked to see how adorable he was.

Scott was three and Joey was five when I got a job as the secretary at our church. Having no car, I would put both boys in the basket of my bicycle and, dressed in office attire and high heels, would peddle us all to the church. There, two different buses would pick each boy up and take them to their respective schools. Joel attended the Dale Evans Rogers School for retarded children and Scott went to a local church pre-school. I don't recall how many hours a week I worked but it was good for all of us. It was at the church I discovered Christian testimony books and where I fell deeply in love with my Savior, Jesus Christ.

During break periods, I would sit at one of the pianos and sing to my Lord. I was not really good at either, yet I knew my Lord loved it.

Thankfully, after a couple of weeks of bicycling to work with my boys in tow, my husband came home one day and said, "I have a surprise for you!" He took me by the hand and led me to the driveway where sat this ugly old blue ford. I gulped and tried to act happy. "Oh, honey... you got me a car!!!"

"I know it isn't much but it will get you where you are going!" (was that ever an understatement) he assured me, as we walked around the car. On the passenger side there were big holes in the front door and the back door.

"Why are those holes there?"

He grinned sheepishly, "Well, this was a painter's "truck" and there is where he hooked his ladder." Oh, well! that just makes perfect sense!!! I looked at the inside and sure enough it was old. The floor board in back seat on the driver's side had a big hole. When I looked through it, I could see the ground. I immediately thought about boys shoes being forever lost through that hole. He assured me that was an easy fix. My sweet husband was so proud that he had found me a car, I soon was able to appreciate it. He did, after all, pay a whole $50.00 for it. So now I had wheels. And he did repair the hole in the floorboard. The boys and I would sing at the tops of our lungs as we drove about in our car. Amazingly, Joey couldn't sing words but he always had the melody.

April 12, Scott's fourth birthday; he looked quite cute in his striped t-shirt and tan shorts. Excited wasn't nearly a strong enough word to describe the joy my little boy was feeling. His wish for his birthday was a wheelbarrow. He loved working in the yard with his dad. He already had a rake and shovel. All he needed to make him completely happy was a wheelbarrow, and he was having his very first birthday party. We had gone through all the elements of the party and now the kids were all playing out in the back yard.

I was in the kitchen when Joey walked over and pulled on my skirt. I picked him up and we sat in one of the kitchen chairs. He laid his head on my shoulder and began to cry. He cried and cried as I held him there in my arms. Somehow, I knew why he was crying. It was the only time I ever saw Joel feeling sorry that he wasn't able to keep up with all the kids playing in the back yard. He had no words to explain this to me, but I feel the Lord just allowed me to see into his heart for that moment and I cried with him. That was the only time I ever remember him crying for himself. When he climbed down off my lap, the smile was back and he went back to doing what he did best…. looking through his Bible.

Oklahoma City Froese's
1965

Denver

1967 Allen's company transferred him to the Denver office of Trailmobile Semi Trailer Company. We were so excited about moving. We would truly be on our own and away from the close reach of our families. The movers came and packed us up, and we said our sad good-byes to my family. Joey and I got in my old blue Ford and Allen and Scott took the lead in our new VW Beetle and we were off to Colorado. No friends or family to help take up the slack…just a little family of four moving to one of the most beautiful cities in the United States.

Allen was warned by his new manager that when it gets cold outside in Colorado it isn't like Oklahoma. It isn't humid but rather a dry cold. It doesn't freeze you to the bone but, sometimes, the sun shining on the snow can fool you. You must wear an overcoat because in this kind of cold weather you can get hypothermia easily. The snow was so gorgeous. The boys loved to play outdoors. We loved to look outside on winter mornings to see the ice frozen on the trees and big icicles hanging from the eaves.

One day we took off for the mountains; our aim to find out all about snow skiing. We drove into a ski resort and looked for a place to park. "Oh, my gosh! Look!" I exclaimed. A skier came down off the slope, careened right in front of us and came to rest, head-first in a gully. We held our breath until we saw him slowly right himself. Allen and I looked at each other and said, "Don't think we'll try skiing." And off we drove.

We became active Westminster Baptist church. After the morning service, Joel would make a b-line to the pulpit and would gabber into the microphone until someone turned it off. The first time I saw him do that I was flabbergasted and embarrassed, but then, as I began to watch him Sunday after Sunday, I knew he was very serious about what he was doing and saying. We didn't understand, but I know His Father understood.

Joel's eyes were always a puzzlement to me. They were so clear and full of understanding. Most "retarded children's" eyes show their diminished cognition. This made his lack of speech that much more perplexing. His teachers in Denver were very positive about his involvement in his schooling; others saw the intelligence. He quickly learned his ABCs. In those days, there was such limited funding for handicapped children. They held classes in an old, worn-out school building that was no longer in use. We didn't care. We were just happy he had a place.

Allen was a workaholic. I finally laid down the law, "Either you are here for breakfast or you are here for dinner. The boys never get to see you!" He knew he had been neglecting all of us, so one day he surprised us by bringing home one of Scott's deep desires. A dog! A beagle we named Snipper. We all loved that little dog and the boys spent lots of time enjoying him.

One day, Joey locked himself in the bathroom. The door was a little tricky and I guess he hit it the wrong way and it locked. I was totally panicked, pounding on the door, "Joey, you open this door right this minute!!!" All the while knowing he didn't know how to turn the lock on the doorknob.... I was pacing back and forth – praying out loud when Scott came in. "What happened?"

"Joey's locked himself in the bathroom and I don't know how to get him out!"

"Don't worry, mom, I'll fix it." He found a screwdriver in the tool drawer and proceeded to take the door knob apart. I stood there amazed. My little boy was only in kindergarten and he knew what to do! From that moment, he became my go - to guy when something needed fixing.

One sunny, summer day, I realized the boys had been playing in the backyard for a long time and I hadn't checked on them. Earlier that morning I asked Scott what he was going to do that morning and he said, "I'm going to dig a big hole to keep my fish in when dad and I go fishing." I encouraged him to have fun. Now I went to check on them. I saw Scott, but didn't see Joey.

"Scotty, where is Joey?"

"He's right here, mom!"

I walked across the backyard and looked into this huge crater he had dug...and there sat Joey and Snipper at the bottom of it. "What in the world have you done?"

"I told you I was going to dig a hole!"

"Honey, I thought you were going to dig a little hole!"

Those boys played in that hole for days. Allen took Scott fishing that week-end and they bought home some carp. Scott couldn't wait to get to the backyard.

Joe was a little shocked!

Scotty filled that huge hole with water and put those fish in it. Well, naturally the fish died and the hole stank like nothing else but rotten fish….but he had a great experience. It wasn't nearly as much fun when dad said he had to fill that hole back in with dirt.

One day Allen came in from work with a wicked grin on his face and said we were moving to California.

"What!" my heart sank to my toes.

The boys were well adjusted, we loved our house, I was on the Governor of Colorado's Commission on Mental Retardation to bring more help for the mentally handicapped. Scott was doing well in kindergarten. And we had been told that after living with the Rocky Mountains as a backdrop in our daily lives, we'd never be happy away from them.

Alas, those were the days before a wife could negotiate with her husband about such matters, so the movers came in and packed us up and off we went.

I and Joey and our dog, Snipper were in my old blue Ford and Allen & Scott in our VW Bug. We traveled in February and it was freezing cold. At one point, as we passed over Donner Pass, the snow was piled up on either side of the road about twenty feet high. It was so snowy and blowing that you could hardly see where you were going. I saw the VW Bug veer off on a side road and I thought maybe I'd seen the last of half of my family and I laid on the horn. A few minutes later I saw the little bug backing out of the snowy side road. Be still my heart!

My car was so drafty with the repaired hole in the back floorboard. But in its defense, that old car never needed maintenance. Never was in the shop the entire eighteen months we lived in Colorado. It just ran and ran. Allen's VW had to have a lightbulb plugged in under the hood every night to keep from freezing, but mine – every morning I'd hop into it and the engine turned right over. We were getting our money's worth out of that old car, that's for sure!

I'd only been to California once, when Joey was two months old we and we flew out to meet Allen's family who lived in the central valley not far from Fresno, where most of the fruit was grown.

As we were traveling I began to muse as to what we could expect in Northern California. Allen's office was in the outskirts of Oakland. I felt sure all the women wore mink stoles and high heels; smoking cigarettes out of rhinestone holders. There probably won't be any churches or people who love God. It's going to be Sodom and Gomorrah all over again! Was I ever wrong!

Hayward, CA

We were about frozen to the bone when we pulled into northern California, The house we rented was in Hayward and the eighteen months we lived there I never got warm.

The first day we were in our house, Scott discovered snails. These little creatures were everywhere. He thought they were amazing and would collect them in cans. We quickly found out how California people felt about them. They would pour salt on them or just stomp on them. We thought this was so cruel.

In our new back yard was the most marvelous tree. I had never seen one like it. The flowers looked just like the brush all mothers use to wash their baby bottles. This tree just astounded me! God had created a tree with the most unusual blooms. I could imagine some mother looking at one of those trees at the same time she was pondering the best way to clean her baby's bottle. and wala…right before her was the answer. I believe God has a wonderful sense of humor and knew someone would get the message or inspiration so He just made an entire beautiful species of tree to fill that need.

The first thing we did after unpacking was to find a church. We were so delighted to find Elmhurst Southern Baptist Church within walking distance of our new home. We quickly made friends and settled into a new routine.

As Christians, it is a wonderful thing that when you move into an unfamiliar environment, as soon as you find a new church you are surrounded by family. As a young couple, Allen and I loved to work with the teen-agers at church and soon our home was filled with laughing, joking kids. Joey and Scott thrived and felt loved and accepted by them. Sandy Sherfy, one of the youth in our church, lived across the street from us and she became our babysitter. She loved the boys and she also loved dressing up in my wedding gown. I'll never forget the day she said, "I have to show my mom!" and she ran across the street with the train of my dress billowing out behind her.

Joey loved to walk, or to be more exact – trot, down the sidewalk with his red wagon in tow. He was a precious sight for any mother to behold. By now he was really tall. He still wore a bib and with one hand stuck in his mouth, for support, he and the wagon would fly down the sidewalk.

His schooling again focused on his ABC's. Since he wasn't verbal, his teachers didn't know how much he knew or understood…so where ever we went they began all over again with the ABC's.

I was so thrilled that at our church, two women began a Sunday School class just for Joey. A photographer from the local paper even came out and did an article about the class for mentally challenged children. Our church was hopeful other parents in the Hawyard area would bring their children, but no one ever did. Joey thrived on all that attention.

One of the teachers at Joey's school told us there was a Cub Scout troupe for Joel's age, for those with special needs. I quickly enrolled him. He was so excited to go to meetings in a Cub Scout uniform. He looked adorable in that navy-blue beanie with the yellow scarf around his neck.

Yearly, since we moved away from Oklahoma City and my mom and dad, I would take the boys on the train to visit them once a year. We always stayed between a month and six weeks - long enough for them to get so sick of us they wouldn't mind our leaving. I found that was a pretty good strategy.

One year, it was time to go back to California after such a visit. Mother and daddy boarded the train with us in Oklahoma City, just long enough to help us get situated with the luggage. With a lurch, the train began to move. We hadn't heard the ALL CLEAR call, at all. My daddy started swearing up a blue streak. I'm trying to calm him down and he's yelling for the conductor. Finally, the conductor comes down the aisle and says, "What's the trouble?"

Daddy yells, "Let me of this $#%^ train!"

"Sir, I'm sorry to tell you but this train won't stop until the next town," replied the conductor.

Now daddy starts up even worse @@##$@##$%$#@@. Mother and I are cracking up. I look at her. She doesn't have her purse. She has her house shoes on and just a wrap-around house dress. We finally get daddy into a seat and quietened down so we could think what we should do. By this time, the entire train car knows what is going on and everyone is hooting. The conductor doesn't think it's funny at all but tells us how much it will cost for them to take the next train back to Oklahoma City. I give it to them from the cash I have. When we pull into the first station and they get off the train, they look at us through the window and we all wave...but this time instead of parting in tears we are all laughing hysterically – except for my dad. Even the boys thought this was a very funny little adventure. If it hadn't been for mother, I'm sure my daddy would have started walking down the railroad tracks.

Allen loved to surprise us with presents when we returned home. He really seemed to miss us, but I knew it was also his time to shop for things he wanted and would say he got them for me. But that was fine with me. This particular time, it was a new car. He bought a new tomato red VW Hatchback and I inherited the VW Bug. I was so thrilled to finally be shed of the old blue Ford, which, by the way, still ran perfectly. I told one of my friends I was going to sell it. She said, "I want it! What do you want for it?" I said, surprised. I couldn't imagine anyone wanting to drive it!

"Well, I guess I'd sell it for $50.00." She didn't bat an eye and gave me the money. That car had taken me all over Oklahoma City, Denver, and to California and I sold it for what we paid for it. Despite my feelings for that old blue ford, it treated me very well! And my new car - Allen told me it didn't take water in the engine, and I thought he said it didn't take oil - so I burned the motor completely out of it. It was a good while before we could afford to repair it, so I was carless again! Sure wished I hadn't sold the old blue ford.

My friend, Mary Jane and I started a women's Bible Study in my home and we were studying healing. I began to ask the Lord to heal Joel. "Father, Joey brought us to know you. Allen and I have been faithful to follow you, so Lord, would you please heal him."

During those days of our prayer group learning about divine healing, Katherine Kuhlman, who had a renowned healing ministry, was holding meetings in Sacramento, so Mary Jane and I decided to take Joey to one of her meetings, feeling sure that he would be instantly healed.

We stood in line for hours to get into the auditorium. We sat through her incredible meeting which lasted for hours. All around us people were jumping up, saying they were healed of their afflictions. People came out of wheelchairs, threw canes down, had their ears and eyes opened… yet we drove home terribly disappointed. Joey was his same sweet, drooling self. After several other instances where I'd taken him to receive special prayer I was dejected. One day the Lord spoke to my spirit through His Word. "My Grace is sufficient for you!" That was it! All it took for me to be able to turn Joey over to God. "Yes, My God. Your Grace is SUFFICIENT FOR ME AND MY FAMILY!" I never again entertained the thought that Joel would be healed on this earth.

Heaven had now become real to the Froese family. We could see with spirit eyes what he would someday be and that was enough for us. A huge load was lifted from our little family and we were, in fact, truly healed.

Allen continued to work way too much, but by now was a deacon in our church. I sold Avon while the boys were in school. We were very busy people.

Then, one day – AGAIN! - about a year and a half into our time in Hayward, Allen came home and said we needed to talk. "I've been offered a job managing a small trucking company in Vista. It's in southern California. It's in a small town. I know I've been working way too much and this may be my way out. What do you think?"

Wow! what did I think???? He continued, "The owner wants me to come down and look the place over, look at the town, get the lay of the land before I make a decision."

"This time I didn't balk. If it would mean him working less I was all for it. Well, of course, you have to go!" I replied.

A couple of days later he made the trip. When he called me from Vista he said, "Babe, you will love it here! It is a small town of 37,000 people. There are mountains in the background. It is beautiful."

Naturally, he took the job.

Home At Last!

This time we had to move ourselves. We found a lovely house to rent in a very remote area of Vista. At the end of moving day Allen said, "Okay, this is it. We are never moving again!" Allen was a man of few words. When he spoke, it was gospel to his little family. Luckily the people from whom we rented were willing to sell us the house and we never moved again. We lived there the rest of Allen's life, some 40 years. Our home had a fabulous view of hills and mountains and we could see all the way to the ocean - some nine miles away. On a really clear day we could see Catalina Island on the far distant horizon. And the sunsets were spectacular. We had a half acre lot and at the back of the house, just across the wide varenka (gully), was a large chicken ranch. Naturally, as we moved in, we had the doors wide open. At the end of moving day, I'd never seen flies as big as the ones that were thick at our windows. Ugh! A housewarming present from our neighbor across the gully! It took days before we got shed of them.

Our boys were eight and ten when we arrived.

Our house was so difficult to find that each of us had to carry a map when we went out, in order to find our way home. Always, when we had out of town guests, we had to meet them at a gas station and lead them to the house. It was a beautiful place to live however, and we were so happy in our new home.

We found excellent schools for them both and there were school buses for each.

Our neighbors were very friendly and one couple came to call just a day or two after our arrival. They invited us to visit their church and we attended there the next Sunday. Since it was a Southern Baptist Church, we joined immediately. I hadn't seen a single mink stole or anyone smoking a cigarette from a rhinestone cigarette holder since coming to California....and there were several Christian stations on the radio. All was good.

While Scott rode his bike on the dirt roads around our house, Joey started walking the area, pulling his red wagon. One afternoon the boys were both out roaming the neighborhood. Scott came home and I said, "Where's Joey?"

"I don't know Mom, he wasn't with me," Scott replied. I went outside and started calling him. No answer! Scott took off again on his bicycle to look. I ran down the roads leading toward the mountain and he was nowhere in sight. I called Allen, "Honey, Joel went out with his red wagon about an hour ago and I can't find him."

He said, "Okay, just stay calm. I'll be right home." I alerted the neighbors and we all began searching for him. The sun was beginning to set and I was panicky. There were coyotes and bob cats in the surrounding hills. We called the sheriff and told the deputy what had happened. He alerted the patrol cars. By now it was almost dark. It had been several hours of intense combing the hills and roads and we hadn't turned up anything. I was at home waiting.

I was praying and crying when a sheriff's car drove into the driveway. I flew out the front door! The deputy opened the back door to his cruiser and there sat Joey. He was filthy dirty, arms and face scratched and bloody. "Thank you God!" was all I could think of!

The deputy said, "I found him walking down East Vista Way, in the middle of the road, out by the Country Kitchen."

"What!" I was incredulous. How could that be! It was at least a mile down to Vista Way and all the way out to the Country Kitchen was another half mile.

"I think he must have cut cross country, down the hill, and through the brush, judging from the scrapes on his face and arms," replied the deputy.

I thanked him from the bottom of my heart. He told me he would alert the people out searching for Joey that he was safe. And I took my tired, bloody little boy to the bathtub. I was alternately telling him how much I loved him and thanking God for bringing him home and screaming at him that he better NEVER do that again. He, sitting in a tub of suds, just looked at me with tears rolling down his cheeks. My God! I had never been so scared.

The next Sunday at church I gave testimony, during the morning service, of God's faithfulness to our family. After the service, a couple came up to me and said, "You know, we were driving down East Vista Way the other day and saw Joey walking beside the road. We wondered what he was doing way out there!" That was it! That's all they said!! I was shocked, speechless.

It took me a long time, to forgive that couple for their unwillingness to become involved. We never did find Joey's red wagon.

Joel's Time

In the 1970's, Special Olympics was just being formed in our part of the country and I was excited to see if Joey could participate in any of the events. By this time, he was about thirteen. I began to take him to some of the events and we saw people far more impaired than he; running, throwing balls, playing floor hockey. He was anxious to join them. He attended California Avenue School in Vista and had learned academically, but at home, I continued to do everything for him. I anticipated his needs: giving him a glass of water if I thought he might be thirsty; putting his clothes on him; brushing his teeth. He could feed himself and go to the bathroom by himself except I had to wipe his bottom. Since he had limited fine motor skills and couldn't put his fingers together, but rather gripped with this whole hand, I never dreamed he would be able to actually dress himself. He looked very intelligent from his eyes, but never spoke. Oh, he was vocal alright; jabbering, laughing at jokes and singing at appropriate times but he wasn't able to form words with his mouth that anyone could understand.

I slowly began to realize that if he was ever going to develop to his full potential it would have to be away from me. It was a terribly painful thought; however, I believe God planted that thought into my head, but I wasn't near ready to act on it.

When he was fifteen years old, I got a call from Regional Center for the Developmentally Disabled. The social worker asked me, "Are you ready to place Joel? there is an opening at the Home of the Guiding Hand in Lakeside, CA. and I believe Joel would be a good fit."

This was a distance of about an hour from our home. Am I ready? God!!! Can I let go of my precious one??? I cried out to Him. To this day, I can still feel the deep gut level panic, I felt at that question. We had loved and protected Joel all of his life... Oh God!!! What if someone mistreated him. A million thoughts ran through my head!!! The agony of that decision!

Yet, I think the last outing we had all tried to do as a family showed us that we also had Scott, our younger son, to consider. Scott, Allen, and I had all decided we'd like to try hiking up and around the mountains that ringed two sides of our home. The four of us put on our best walking shoes and set out one morning with our bottles of water. I think we made it until noon before we were all worn out trying to drag Joel over rocks and boulders. He could walk faster than any of us but he couldn't navigate rough terrain and by this time he was squawking loudly at being dragged here and there. We all sat on rocks and drank our water and laughed about how, at least, we wouldn't need to buy hiking boots.

Scott had always loved his brother so much – also loved to make him squeal! He would tease him until I'd threaten to bop him if he didn't quit.... but Scott was now thirteen and we wanted to have some time to devote to just him.

So, here it was. The time we had all been dreading so much. A couple of days prior to Joel's move to the Home of Guiding Hands, as we were making final arrangements, a staff member had said to me, "We would like you not to contact Joel for the first six weeks he is with us. Just to give him time to adjust to his new home. But, please feel free to call us and we'll let you know how he's doing."

When we took Joel down to HGH, we knew we were facing a major separation. Six weeks! The four of us walked around and met all the staff and residents and were reassured that they were glad Joel was there and everyone would do everything they could to make him feel at home. I put all his pictures on the wall in his third of the room. I carefully placed his clothes into his bureau, his books and his Bible on top of the bureau and his clothes in his closet – lingering as long as possible. When the moment came for us to leave our hearts…at that place, Joel cheerfully said, "Bye!" As the door closed behind us, Allen had to hold me up to get me in the car.

The three of us cried all the way home. Even though those were financially lean times for us, as we neared Vista, Allen said, "You know what! I think we should go to Love's." This was our favorite restaurant. Through the years this bar-b-que restaurant had been the scene of many family celebrations …. so - we were going to try to celebrate! And we did through our tears.

Later, as we walked into our home, there was a huge void all around us. The "quiet" screamed at us. However, Scott now had his own room. I could sleep through the night, without one ear being attuned to Joel's needs. It was all good, but it really was hard on our hearts.

After couple of days passed, I could stand it no longer. I called Joe's quad at HGH and with a knot in my throat said, "Hi, this is Joey's mom. How is he doing?"

"Well, let me tell you. Joel can now dress himself!"

"What!"

"Yes mam! We laid his clothes out on his bed and said Joe, when you get hungry put your clothes on and you can come out and eat!"

"What!"

"Yes mam! Two days later he was out of his room, fully dressed."

I was stunned! She also added, "You know what! Your son is so happy here, I think it would be fine if you came on down to see him. He is really doing great!" I hit the road in no time flat. And when I arrived she was RIGHT.... He was so glad to see me, showing me all around the grounds. There was a garden, a plant nursery where many of the older residents worked, a large recreation building, a chapel and they had their own chaplain. There was lots of positive, happy activity all around the place. When it was time for me to go home, I hugged Joel tight and he said brightly, "Bye Mom!"

My heart sang this time as I drove home. "God you are such a GREAT AND AWESOME FATHER."

We started out bringing Joel home every other week-end, and at the end of six months or so we began car-pooling with another family from Vista. That made life a lot easier. I only had to drive one way. He was at home for all the holidays and summer vacations.

Of course, there were things that really bugged me about where he lived. We labeled every stitch of clothes, shoes, etc., but I'd buy him something new and that is the last I'd see of it. It was like "putting money down a rat hole!" I knew the staff did the best they could, but when he'd come home with shoes on that were two sizes too big or too small, that was tough.

About a year after Joel moved to HGH, I had him to his pediatrician and he said, "Have you ever thought about taking care of Joel's drooling." All of his life, when he got a little anxious or studious he would put his hand into his mouth and the drooling was excessive. We had just learned to live with it and even now he wore a bib to keep his shirt dry.

"You mean something could be done to help him?"

"Yes, It's called drool surgery. We make a tiny incision on either side of his lower jaw and snip the saliva glands. It might cause him to have a dry mouth, but you could encourage him to drink more water," the doctor instructed me.

"Yes, yes. yes!! Let's do it!" I was thrilled. An appointment was made for the procedure to be done at Children's Hospital and it only required one overnight. When I brought him home the next day he looked like someone had socked him in both jaws but there were no more bibs. What an amazing difference!

Joel also had a wonderful dentist, Dr. Mary O'Conner, such a God-send to the handicapped population. Located in San Diego, her office was such a joyous place to go. The little Down Syndrome kids were so happy and joyful. Kids in wheelchairs or walkers had a place just for them. The office was bright and full of fun. The Doctor and all her staff wore fun scrubs and each kid left there with a new toy. Dr. Mary rounded a bunch of her patients, about twice a year, for those who needed crowns, root canals, or fillings. She made arrangements with a local hospital to do outpatient surgery, putting her patients under general anesthetic to take care of all their dental problems. The only cost we ever incurred was when we asked her to cap all of Joel's teeth. This was costly but Joel was such a handsome man, I didn't want his mouth to be a distraction. Dr. Mary was amazing… still is today. She inherited her practice from her dad. He had a real heart for the handicapped.

Joel was about eighteen when his doctor said he thought his scoliosis was sever enough that it was time to think about Harrington Rods. Harrington Rods have been used for some years as a last resort for curvature of the spine, damaged vertebra, etc. After insertion, the tissue would grow around the rods, inserted on both sides of the spine, shoring the spine straight. The doctor cautioned me that this surgery was very serious and would require Joel wearing a body cast for at least six months. Oh, God!! What should we do?

Allen and I discussed it thoroughly and finally decided that it had to be done. We contacted his caregivers at HGH and they assured us that they were up to whatever care he might require, post-surgery. So, the date was set. I guess it didn't really occur to me just how serious the procedure was, until the day of surgery when the anesthesiologist called me out into the hallway. "We will have to stop all his natural life force and will keep him alive by machine as we do the surgery. It should be fine. We have a great team of doctors!" This was before the days of heart and limb transplants and the amazing surgeries they now do…To stop all life function was SERIOUS!!!

"GOD!!!" I cried in my spirit.

I was crying when I called Allen at his office. "Honey, I need you!!! This surgery is BAD!" We had already discussed that he wasn't going to be able to come because his business was going through their yearly audit and as the business manager he had to be there to give any figures the auditors might require. But now I really needed him. Again, he had to tell me he couldn't come. I dried my tears and said, "Okay, come when you can."

My precious son was in ICU for days. I stayed right by his side. At night I would go to the car to try to sleep for a few hours as there was no place for me in the hospital. He left the hospital in a molded body cast from his chin to his buttocks.

He was delivered to HGH by ambulance. As we were unloading him, the staff assured me that they were his family also and they could take as good a care of him as I would. They assured me that they would call and give me updates. "Mary, you go on. He'll be fine." By this time I was working at the Carlsbad Chamber of Commerce in Carlsbad, California and I had been off work as long as I was allowed.

One last kiss and my boy looked up at me and said, "Bye, mom!" I could hardly bear to leave him...again.

"Thank you, God!" was my weary mantra all the way home after an incredibly hard, long week. For Joel it was only the beginning of a LONG ordeal. Six months of wearing a cumbersome body cast. No baths, no showers. A sponge bath for six months, yuck! And Lakeside is very warm in summer. He could walk well enough, after he got the hang of the extra weight. Thankfully, school was out for the summer, which was a very good thing.

I knew no one at HGH would think to stick a knitting needle down his front and back to give him a good scratch...but that was one of the things mama did for him when he'd come home for the week-end. As he sat to eat, he could hardly see his plate as the cast was up to his neck, with only a cut-out to allow for his adams apple. He had little room to swallow his food. It was just a bad scene, but he never complained.

Finally, the day came we'd all been waiting for. The cast was cut off. He had a long purple scar from above his shoulder blade to his buttocks but it all had healed nicely. He was never supposed to be able to bend over from the waist; however, Joel didn't know that. His back might be stiff but he was going to bend over. Over time, a large protrusion, just a large knot really, formed at the base of the rods but it worked for him.

We had always told Joel he was our angel. When he would see a photo of an angel he always associated with it. One week-end when he was home he was sitting in the living room reading his Bible when he jumped up and ran into the kitchen. "Look, Mom, here's me in the Bible." I looked where he was pointing. It was Exodus 23:20. "Behold, I send my angel before you to keep you in the way and bring you into the place I have prepared for you." I was shocked.

"Wow, Joe! I didn't know that was in the Bible. It looks just like you!" I thought it was a wonderful Scripture but I also thought it was just a flook... We knew he could spot read words and we'd always told him he was our angel, but this! The next day in Sunday School I said, "Joel, do you think you could find that Scripture again?"

"Es!" and he turned right to it. I was amazed. I told Allen and Scott when we were at lunch after church. Joel just beamed. That has been our life verse. Throughout his life I've said, "Joel will you find our verse for me." And he always turned right to it. That verse has kept me stable at some very bad times through the years. He truly was the guiding force in our family. He kept us up close in our devotions. Every time he was home, before the meals, he would pass out the Bibles and off we'd go. And Heaven – oh, it's became so real to us! For we all talked about how fun it would be for Joel to be able to run and jump and do all the things he couldn't do while on this earth.

Joel and the other high schoolers from HGH were bussed to El Cajon High School for their TMR (trainable mentally retarded) program. Students were allowed to stay in school until they were twenty-one before they "graduated." I would visit the school from time to time and I was so impressed with my son's teachers and their patience with this population. He had one teacher who particularly loved him – Mrs. Veira. One day, after he'd been at HGH for about three years she called me and said, "Mary, there is a new Group home opening in Lakeside and I want Joel to live there!"

"WOW!! Really!"

"Yes, it's a young couple who have two kids in elementary school and she wants to do this so she can stay home and raise her kids, instead of working outside the home. She is a real DIN A MO!!! I think this would be a great place for Joel!"

"Well, of course, if you recommend it, I'll take a look!"

"Mary, please hurry…this home will fill up fast, believe me!!!"

She gave me the phone number and I called immediately. Kathy answered the phone and her enthusiasm just jumped right on to me over the phone. We made arrangements for me to bring Joel over to see her family. I was petrified. What if I take Joe out of HGH and we lose our place….and this young woman decides this is a bigger commitment than she wants.

The day came for the interview and I picked Joel up from HGH. He had the most horrible cold I'd ever seen on him. Joel couldn't sniff his nose. When it ran, he couldn't wipe it with a tissue... IT JUST RAN... DOWN TO HIS MOUTH!!! YUCK!! and DOUBLE YUCK!!! All the time Kathy was showing us around, I had to keep a tissue under his nose and a couple of times it got away from me and she saw it. I thought to myself, if she wants Joel after this episode, even though I'd assured her I'd never seen anything like this on him before, I'd be amazed.

Joel & John were roommates for twenty years.

The Jardine home was really lovely. It was high on a hill in Lakeside. There were no neighbors and the view from their beautiful swimming pool was spectacular. The inside of the house was extremely nice; a large family room, a formal living room, their own children's rooms and two client bedrooms and a master bedroom on one side of the house and on the other side they had made their garage into a bedroom, an office and another bathroom and utility room.

That is the room Joel would share with John, the only other client they had at the time. John was autistic and about Joel's age and he'd already been there about a month. He liked it there and he didn't want anyone else to be there! So, when Kathy introduced him to Joel, John took off out the back door and slammed it hard behind him. Kathy said, "Don't worry about John...he'll come around." John was a very handsome young man. Looking at him at first you'd never know there was a problem. He just had difficulty connecting with people. He had no family to look after him so he became very attached to his new family.

While we were at the Jardine home that day we got to meet Kathy's husband, Bob, their eight year old son, Todd, and six year old Jenny. They assured me that they had prayed and planned for this home for some time. When Kathy was growing up her mother had the same type of business in their home, so Kathy really understood what she was getting into. She assured me they were committed Christians and everyone would be going to church on Sundays. They went to the now famous, Shadow Mountain Church in El Cajon. David Jeremiah was the pastor.

After Joel and I left, the Jardine family discussed Joel being a part of their family and all agreed they thought he would fit in nicely with their family. I went home and talked it over with Allen. We agreed also, so we took a huge leap of faith and said, "Okay, we'll move him over at the first of the month." Joel lived with the Jardine family, which enlarged to include six more residents, all girls, almost twenty-five years and John was his roommate that entire time. Jennie, the little girl who loved to play with Joey when she was six and seven and eight, became a lovely, compassionate woman who now has a family of her own, but she always loved Joel.

Kathy told me they would be an active family and that was an understatement. Part of the Jardine's job was mainstreaming their clients as much as possible. (I always hated that name (client) and so did Kathy. To her they were her kids but that was the legal term she was required to use in public). They were in Special Olympics one night a week and once a month they went to an entire week-end meet. They had season tickets to the Padres Games, they went to the Old Globe Theatre, Sunday School, and they took fantastic vacations. They went to dude ranches, Walt Disney World in Florida….Disneyland California was a yearly event. It just made my head swim to think of the activity level of this household. Joel continued to come home one week-end a month and all the holidays, and summer vacations.

Graduation

In 1981, Joel graduated from high school. What a big event for all of us!!! In California the developmentally disabled are allowed to continue in public school until they are twenty-one. Graduation Day came for Joel and several of his friends at the Jardine Home. Joel had a new suit and proudly walked across the stage to receive his diploma, when his name was called. As always, he looked over the crowd for his beaming mom and there I was.

The girls had on lovely long dresses and corsages. A dance was held afterward where everyone celebrated with great gusto. I loved to go to their dances because all the Downs Syndrome boys and girls were so "Hip." They could dance up a storm as they seen done on television on American Bandstand. The entire group went to Disneyland for their "senior trip." I didn't hear until much later that Joel got "Lost!" for hours. We had learned years earlier that when we took Joel somewhere like an amusement park, we had to put him in a wheelchair so we could keep up with him. Once he started walking as a four year old, he ran. Now as a young adult he could boggy!

In several visits home I had noticed that Joel had begun to snore terribly. You could hear him all over the house. I thought to myself, that just isn't normal. I made an appointment with a specialist to look at his nose. The doctor took a quick look up his nasal passage and said, "He has a deviated septum." He made an appointment for surgery immediately. We were there bright and early on surgery day. The doctor said it was a very quick process, so go have coffee and we'll be finished shortly. I waited and waited. It didn't seem like a quick process to me. Finally, the doctor came out and said they had run into something a little out of the ordinary. He had a tumor about six inches long right behind his septum. The doctor said, "He should be breathing good in a few days. We have his nose all packed with dressing. There is a straw placed in the middle of the packing on either side. He should be able to breathe through them until we take the packing out. Be sure he sleeps sitting up for the next few nights and above all, do not let him take the packing out!"

Joel came out of recovery and sure enough his nose was packed. We got in the car and started home. I told him how important it was that he not touch his nose. When we got home, I got him in the bathroom to get him ready for bed. I had to leave the room for a minute and I again reminded him, "Joel, please don't touch your nose...it's really important." I ran out to do what I needed to do and when I got back ALL the packing was in the sink. Joel sat on the toilet with his nose dripping blood. I screamed and hollered at him but it didn't do a bit of good, the deed had been done.

I immediately called the doctor and asked him what I should do. He said, "WELL…I guess it will be okay. It should quit bleeding soon. Just keep him sitting up to sleep and we'll see what happens." Wow, trumped again! We both sat up in recliners for the next few nights and he did okay.

We went for the follow-up visit with the Dr. he said, "Well, Joel I guess you showed we don't have to have all that packing!" From that time forth, Joel slept like a baby with no snoring.

Floor Hockey

One Friday evening I received a call from Kathy telling me Joel would be participating in Special Olympics Games that were being held in Fallbrook, a neighboring town, on Saturday morning.

On this day, I am so excited because most of the time they are so far away I don't have opportunity to attend. This time I get to see my boy play floor hockey.

The squeaking and squealing of sneakers against the wooden gym floor put my teeth on edge as I slipped through the gym door. I had no idea what to expect and was not prepared for the noise level. Loud cheers echo off the walls of the hockey teams in their colorful uniforms. I stand at the door and try to see my son…finally I spot him.

He and his team are sitting up on the stage area of this multi-purpose gym. I try to move out of sight before he sees me. I want to see him interact with his team, but no such luck. He spots me and darts across the stage toward me hollering. "Mom, mom….hi mom!" How I love the sound of those familiar faltering words.

There we sit, side by side, feet dangling over the edge of the stage, watching the action. Those playing at the moment are in the higher-functioning division, several with Down Syndrome, and they are good! With both teams equally matched, the opponent's strain and fight for control of the puck. Sweat pours down their faces and they grunt like the pros. A goal is made and both sides cheer. Competitiveness is replaced with honest joy in each player's success. High Fives are given all around. There is so much celebrating that the buzzer sounds before they ever get another play in. At the end of the game helmets are pulled off sweaty heads; arms are raised in victory and the cheering is deafening. Each player gives and receives hugs from coaches and players alike. It is a splendid day in Fallbrook at the Special Olympics meet.

Now it's time for my son's team. I watch with a thrill as my lanky 26 year old son puts on his helmet and grabs the hockey stick the coach holds out. "See me Mom!" *Yes, my darling son, I see you with my heart full of love!* He has a sloppy gate due to his mild cerebral palsy. He walks and runs but it is anything but smooth. His coach is giving him some instructions about how to hold the puck. Probably the same instructions he has given him for countless meets. "Joe, remember when you have the puck you run down the court! Put you hockey stick on the floor, don't swing it around in the air….okay, everyone, have fun!"

The buzzer sounds but nobody moves! The players stand idle, sticks in hand, puck on the floor. Couches begin to holler, "Okay, you guys, get the puck, get the puck." "Joe, take your stick and hit it - MOVE!"

Bobby ambles toward the puck and manages to put his stick on it. The coach yells, "Push it, Bobby! Come on, Bobby, you can do it; PUSH!!! That's the way, keep going; push, Bobby, Push!" Bobby looks at his coach, transfers his stick to his weak hand, grins and waves the free hand. Bobby is the only one on either team who has moved. With deep concentration he moves the puck a few inches and then a few more, while the coach, hunkered down at the sidelines and dripping with sweat, cajoles and encourages, willing Bobby to move.

A player from the other team meanders to the puck; gently shoves Bobby's stick away with his own, takes over the puck and inches it in the same direction. His coach yells, "You got it, Scottie! Go the other way….Scotty, turn around. Our goal's on the other end!" And so the game goes. Joe hasn't moved a muscle since he got out on the floor. Neither has anyone else… Finally, the buzzer sounds, ending the first half. Exhausted from mentally trying to help the players move the puck, I observe the coaches. Wringing wet, they encourage their teams. "Great game, guys, you're doing great!!! I'm so proud of you!"

The buzzer sounds for the second half and off they go. Again, the players stand and look at the puck, trying to will their brains to send the proper signals to their hands to move the stick one inch, then one more inch. Finally, Joel, in his stumbling gait, ventures over to the puck and takes control with his stick.

I go crazy, "Come on, Joel, you can do it!" He methodically inches his way along the court and is within range of the goal. The goalie is on the job, guarding the entrance. Joel begins to giggle, causing loss of concentration. He stops to think and again inches the puck along, making time stand still. The coaches jump up and down hollering, "Go for it, Joe; go for it!" Just as the puck is inched into the net the goalie moves into action. In what appears to be slow motion, he steals the puck. Joe turns to me with his impish grin as if to say, "Oh, well, we all did good, huh, Mom!" and the buzzer sounds. Game over.

I'm so exhausted I almost fall off the stage. The players move off the court to their coaches, and players from both teams are welcomed as champions. I look at the coaches. These guys are worn out just trying to get the team to move. Who are these volunteers who care so much for people who are so visibly handicapped? What makes them willing to spend their evenings and week-ends lovingly instructing in such slow-paced learning situations? For years, I have seen the coaches on news clips for Special Olympics. No longer are they nameless faces holding out their waiting arms at the finish lines; today, I see "Special Heroes" who themselves deserve a hug. How do I as a mom of one of these precious athletes say a proper thank you to these men and women? That was a question God heard me ask.

**Joel had the honor of carrying
The Special Olympic torch**

Special Olympic Coaches

I had been writing articles and devotionals for several years and even had some published. I thought maybe I should go to a writers' conference to hone my skills.

One day in 1988, I had jumped in and was attending my first writers conference which was being held at Biola University. I was on my way back to my dorm room when I heard these words, "*It's time to say thank you.*" I looked around to see who had said those words to me, but there was no one there. I continued walking and again heard the words, "*It's time to say thank you!*"

This had not been the most enriching of weeks. By this third day of the conference, I felt like a duck out of water. I could hardly understand what the instructors were talking about. Finally, today, some other ignorant person had asked the question I had been too timid to ask all week. "What is a SASE?" I heard a few giggles from the veteran writers, but I, for one, wanted to hug this guy. The instructor smiled and replied, "It is a self-addressed stamped envelope." I was shocked at my ignorance. I wanted to crawl in a hole.

Now This! "*It's time to say thank you!*"

"Lord, you have spent the last three days here with me, showing me just how ignorant I am and now you are asking me to write a book!!!" Then the Scripture popped into my mind, "My grace is made perfect in weakness."

Then I remembered what God was talking about when He said, *It's time to say thank you.*

I was at the San Diego airport, awaiting the return of a plane full of Special Olympic athletes, including my Joel. They were returning from a week-end at Berkeley University in Oakland, CA. The arrival doors opened and our athletes poured out of the plane. All the parents, caregivers and friends cheered as they deplaned in their uniforms with big, shiny medals around their necks. I was overcome with gratitude for all the exhausted volunteers who came off the plane lugging the items the athletes had left on the plane. Joel and I were arm and arm as we left the airport. I said, "Joel, what was your coaches name?"

"Bob!" was his reply. Just Bob…

I couldn't even send him a thank you card. But I remember saying to myself, "Thank you Bob, you're a Hero of a Special Kind."

As I drove home from the conference God downloaded exactly how to go about writing this book. It was like a movie screen playing in my head as He showed me how to do every phase.

Phase one: Research

He told me write a letter to every Special Olympics organization in each state, asking if they had someone they would like to see honored in a book. I sat down at my computer and the letter wrote itself. I was thrilled when I received the first letter back from one of the organizations. Then came a steady stream of names and addresses. I began to get letters with the names and addresses from each state. He then told me to write each of these coaches a letter and send a cassette tape, asking them to have a cup of coffee and pretend I was there asking them the questions that were wrapped around the tape.

Wonder of all wonders….I got a tape back. I sat down and transcribed the tape… Then others came pouring back into my mailbox. The Lord was so actively involved in this process. He truly showed me every step to take. He told me it would take a year to compile stories and write the book. It would take a year to find a publisher and a year to have it edited and printed. He also told me to write Eunice Kennedy, the founder of Special Olympics, and ask her to do the foreword in the book. I was over the moon when she answered my request.

Phase two: The Publisher

After all the book was completed it was time to find the publisher. I sent it to almost 50 publishing houses. Week after week, I would receive the manuscript back in the SASE I had enclosed. Rejection after rejection came through my mailbox. One day I just laid on the floor talking to God. *Father, I have had such a wonderful time writing the book You have given me.*

It's been one of the highpoints of my life. I've done everything I know to do. I'm not sending out another manuscript. If It's going to get published You are going to have to do it. I'm done!

Within a week one of the publishers that I had already sent the book to called me and asked me to come to Ventura to talk with them. The title of the book was to be, "Heroes of a Special Kind." It was published by

Evergreen Publishers in 1995. Each story was so amazing. Just to think there are more than five hundred thousand volunteers around the world is mind boggling, and more than three million athletes. Every four years, just like regular Olympics, they conduct their international games.

Phase three: The book

My book was introduced at the International Special Olympics Games in Minneapolis, Minnesota. At that time I was able to meet, face- to-face, many of the featured volunteers and their heroes. This was one of the amazing experiences of my life.

At the beginning of the book I told the story of Joel getting off the plane after a week-end at Berkley and walking away from there, frustrated that I couldn't contact Joel's volunteer coach, Bob, to thank him. The SO organization in San Diego was able to find "BOB" a give him a copy of the book. It had come full circle.

Scott

When our second son finished high school, he attended Palomar Community College for a couple of semesters and worked at a fast food restaurant. He had a strong desire to buy land and have a small ranch. He knew he would never be able to accomplish this in California because of the cost of land so when his uncle came to Vista on a visit, Buddy told Scott he could get him a job in Palestine, Texas. Scott thought and prayed about it for several months. After tying up loose ends and selling his horse, he loaded up his pick-up.

On that day in June, 1982, Allen, Scott and I did a group hug and then we prayed for our son's safety in the days ahead. He got into his pick-up and headed out. That was probably the hardest thing his dad and I had ever done, to stand in that driveway and watch as his black Ford pick-up, that he worked and paid for himself, packed with all his worldly goods, drove out of that drive-way.

I had been weeping for weeks at the thought of him leaving us. I never wanted him to see how broken hearted I was, because it is our jobs, as parents, to give our kids the "Wings of the Morning." On that day, I was able to hold it together until we saw that pick-up drive over the crest of the hill and out of sight, and then I just fell apart...

Our boys - our life work- all seemed over in a second. Scott had been such a wonderful son. He had always tried his best. He had always sought to connect with his brother. We never had to deal with the hard things other families had. He'd loved God and sought to please Him in all that he did. But now it was his time. Allen and I walked back into the house, arm in arm. We went into his room that he had just vacated. The room that a year ago we made over into a prospectors shack – complete with burlap at the window and wooden crates nailed to the wall as bookshelves. There on his water bed was a letter addressed to "Mom and Dad." What a precious document. In it he thanked us for allowing him to grow up in an intact family. He said, "I am one of the lucky ones!" His dad and I were also the lucky ones.

Scott did well in his work and within a couple of years he secured his dream. He purchased a house on eight acres in a tiny community, Neches, Texas Population 500. He and his dad became partners in a small cattle herd.

One summer we flew out to see him and Joel was with us. He had such a wonderful time that Scott said he'd love to have Joel come back and spend a week with him, alone. Scott had taken a year off his job to work his ranch and make things for his home and this seemed like an ideal time - Just the two guys. We thought and thought about how we could make this happen. How could Joel get to Texas – alone? To this, I plead temporary insanity!

I allowed Joel, at thirty-two, to fly ALONE to East Texas. He had to change planes in Dallas/Fort Worth to get to his destination of Tyler,

Texas. In planning this trip, I phoned the airlines and told them all about Joel and his many limitations. They assured me they would have a flight attendant at his elbow the entire way, don't worry a bit!

They would wheel chair Joel to his connector flight to Tyler. Joel was still non-verbal. I had a big green pin made, which he wore on his shirt - that told his name, where he lived, the phone number. Everything I could possibly have printed on this pin was there. He carried a little bag with his transistor radio and a few other items to keep him company.

As we stood awaiting the flight, I felt like I might be having a heart attack...my anxiety was so intense. For whatever reason, I had decided to give him a brand new hair-do for the trip. I took his longish, thick light brown hair and combed it straight back. It looked so nice and I sprayed it really stiff so it wouldn't move on him. With lay-over and all, this trip would take about six hours. Of course, he would have to go to the bathroom! I had briefed the airlines of this issue and again they assured me that wasn't a problem. We stood at the departure gate and I passed my precious son off to a flight attendant and reminded God that the angels had better be on their job!!! And I left the airport. I paced the floor that entire day...finally, the phone call came.

Scott hollered into the phone, "**MO–THER**!! I almost didn't claim him! His hair was standing on end - His pants were wet and his face looked like someone had smeared chocolate all over it!" Oh NO!! I had forgotten that Joel had a habit of scratching his head when he got nervous...and his new hair-do was definitely an "OH NO!" Joel was always aware....so he must have been embarrassed at how he looked...I felt like a flop as a mother! But he got to his destination. And, I'm sure they stopped at a bathroom at the airport.

Scott had a circular fence designed to keep the hay away from the cattle, so he had Joel go inside the fence so the cows couldn't crowd him, causing him to fall. In this way, he was able to hand feed the cows carrots, and pellets. He wore a cowboy hat and big boots and so enjoyed himself.

Scott always thought we didn't make Joel do enough work....so he made up for it. In the video he sent us; Joel was pushing the lawnmower, helping his brother hammer some shelves, feeding and watering the cows. They went fishing and did all the things Scott dreamed he would like to do with his brother. They sat on the back porch and ate ice cream in the hot Texas afternoon. It was a wonderful week for both brothers… but then came the trip back to California!!!!

I was so thankful I didn't have to pick him up from the airport… the Jardine's daughter, Jennie, picked him up. Other than let me know he was safely in her hands, she didn't say much about how he looked when he arrived, and I didn't ask. That was definitely a "NEVER AGAIN!" as I thanked God over and over for His divine hand in keeping Joel.

Scott was still single at thirty-eight and very tired. It's very difficult to live such a big dream by yourself. Caring for cattle and eight acres; a home that had no wife; the Neches school district where he was the "go to" man from all things maintenance; and his job at the First Baptist Church of Neches where he was the youth minister. When I told him of a course in Micro-Soft Network Engineering that dad and I would gladly pay for if he thought it would interest him, he jumped at it and within six weeks had sold most of his worldly goods and was on the road to California.

He and his dad had been all-out computer geeks since the early days of home computers. So, this course was really "his thing!" He settled into our guest room and met the challenge of a new career. Almost before we knew it, he had been hired at a huge Southern California School District and was on the campus of the high school, caring for four hundred computers - A different world from a community of 3,000 people in Texas.

Now he commutes daily on a busy freeway.

Has It Really Been 40 years?

Joel's fortieth birthday was approaching. I had always said when Joel leaves earth for heaven we are going to have a huge party…because he is HOME AT LAST. But his dad said, "Why are we waiting for that! Let's have a party now!"

So, the three of us began to plan Joel's birthday bash. In our community there is a major resource for parties, weddings, sixth grade and family camp called Green Oak Ranch. It is a recovery home for drug and alcoholic folk. It is a Christian facility where those in recovery run the many faceted facility. We decided to have Joel's party there and do a western bar-b-que. We invited fifty of our closest friends and family.

It was a beautiful Southern California day. Everyone from his other home came.

By this time – almost 20 years from the time Joel moved in, there were eight mentally handicapped young adults in the family. All of whom piled out of the van ready to party! We had friends from Texas come out and relatives from Central California. What a fun day! Joel was more excited than I'd ever seen him.

The Jardine Clan

The four of us, dressed in denims and cowboy hats, welcomed all of our guests. They arrived with gifts galore! Joel's eyes just sparkled. Our entertainment was a three - piece band named Sunday Shoes.

Joel and I had been practicing his speech before the mirror for days. He was so excited he would just giggle. We'd have to stop and allow him to get control. He'd say a few words and then be reduced to giggles again. But this was his day. This was the day he and his friends were the normal ones. The rest of us just sat back and watched them have the time of their lives.

Joel had wanted to speak into a microphone for years. I remembered those years in Denver when he would make a bee line to the pulpit after service to jabber into the mike. Finally, this was going to happen. Now, here today, he was called to the microphone to make a speech. Of course, I was his interpreter, since I was the only one who could understand him. What a precious few moments as he spoke into the mike through his giggles. He also had to remember to swallow his saliva which always was in danger of getting ahead of him. At the end of the day, Joel had a mountain of new tee shirts, ball caps, and a new Bible.

After all these years, Joel and the other residents of the Jardine home were still very involved with Special Olympics and would go to week-end events once a month. On the week-end they were at one of the local colleges, I was a chaperone. I had charge of Joel and Arlene, a young woman from the Jardine home. She was very short and slow, and her left side was partially paralyzed. Joel, even with his moderate cerebral palsy, could run like the wind.

On this week-end, I was in charge of getting these two from their dorm room to the playing fields. Here we went, Joel running so far ahead I was afraid he'd get lost and Arlene coming at a snail's pace. "Slow down Joe – Hurry up, Arlene" I was a wreck by the time we got to the bocca ball court.

Throughout the week-end, I noticed how frail Joel's skinny body looked. Even with Harrington rods in his back, his scoliosis was causing his back to twist ever more. He had no meat on his bones because of his constant movement, due to his cerebral palsy. I would watch him sit for hours on a hard gym floor and then get up to play his sport. It really looked to me like it was too much for him. It was then that God began to nudge my heart that it was time to bring Joel home to live.

I had been retired for five years or so and I'd done lots of traveling, so I was ready to stay home more. I broached the idea to Allen and he was very reluctant. Caring for Joel was a real job. He had to have help with all his personal needs from brushing his teeth to wiping his bottom. He could dress himself and take himself to the bathroom and feed himself but he had little judgment as to when he was in danger. He couldn't be left home alone. Caring for him WAS a huge task, but I am his mother.

In all the years, as I'd take him back to the Jardine's after his week-end at home, or holiday, it had gotten harder and harder to leave him. Even though Bob and Cathy were wonderful to him, he still wanted to be home. In the last couple of years, I began to wait until Monday morning to return him and would leave him off at his work instead of the Jardine's. Somehow that was easier on both of us.

I truly didn't want to step over my husband's wishes to insist on my own way in this big change in our lives, so I took some time to fast and pray that my heart would come into alignment to his. I told him I would abide with whatever he said, at the end of my fast. It was Sunday morning when I walked up to him and said, "Okay, honey what have you decided?" He waited a few minutes before he said, "Let's bring him home!" I jumped into his arms and wept.

We decided to bring him home on May 27th, his forty-third birthday. Now I had to break the news to his other family that I was breaking up their house. That was one of the hardest things I'd ever had to do and since I'm a coward I wrote them a letter. Cathy was very tearful when she responded. Joel had lived with the Jardine's for more than twenty years. On the day I picked him up they had a going-away birthday party for him at a local pizza place. They did speeches and gave him presents. Cathy said he could come back if it didn't work out at home and we all tearfully parted company.

At home, we had made a big sign for the garage door - "Welcome Home, Joel!" Dad and Scott were there waiting for us as Joel arrived back home to stay.

We're a foursome again!

Joel's Prayers

The first night home I sat on the side of Joel's bed, as I always did, and asked what he wanted to pray about. He thought for a moment and said, "Scott a wife." I almost fell off the bed. Scott had told me at one point, "Mom, if I'm not married by the time I'm forty I probably won't marry, and he was now forty-two. He had been looking for his wife, but in the little country town in Texas where he lived, the girls left home after graduation so there were never any women his age.

When he moved home he had gone back to the Baptist church where he was baptized as a little boy and there were no women there. However, he had just begun attending a huge mega-church in our town and they had a singles ministry.

He never mentioned anything about it so since he was now forty-two, I thought the wife thing was not happening. Now Joel prayed this prayer….AND he prayed the same prayer every single night until the middle of the next January. On this night in January, I sat on his bed and said, "Joel what do you want to pray about?" He replied, "The dog!" I said, "What – you don't want to pray for Scott a wife?"

"No!" Never again did he pray for Scott a wife.

The months passed and it was April and time for Scott's birthday. We were going to take him out for his birthday dinner and he called and said he wanted to bring someone. "Great!!" On the evening of April 12th the front door opened and in came Scott and A BEAUTIFUL WOMAN! My heart began to pound…who is this??? He introduces her as Sarah.

We all go to dinner and as I observe the two of them it dawns on me - they are in love. I felt totally disoriented! How did this happen without me knowing anything about it?? He only lived five minutes away from us.

We had a wonderful evening but as we parted I had a million questions to ask my son. The next day I made a bee line to his house and said, "Scott, when did you meet Sarah.?" He said, "Let me see, we were in a singles Bible study at our church. One evening we all went out to see the Passion of the Christ movie and that's when I really noticed her." I could hardly breathe as I said, "Scott, your brother prayed in your wife!" and I told him the story of Joel's prayers – until the middle of January. Goose flesh raised on both our arms! She was also forty-two. It seems that all the years Scott was in Texas, Sarah was in Los Angeles, working as a social worker and then going back to school to obtain her doctorate in Clinical Psychology. Now God had brought them together.

That summer was an amazing time for our family. They even asked Joel to be their best man at their wedding. This was a dream I'd always had, but it seemed so farfetched…but now, by God's wondrous grace it was happening.

They had a beautiful outdoor wedding at Green Oak Ranch. They stood under the live oak trees surrounded by friends and family, and our family was finally complete –Scott had a wife named Sarah.

BUT, that was only the beginning of Joel's prayers.

Scott and Sarah had been married about two years when, one night as I sat by Joel's bed at prayer time, I said, "Joel, what would you like to pray for tonight?"

He looked at me and smiled, "Scott a baby!" WHAT!!! I was staggered. I had given up hope of ever having a baby in the picture. However, every night it was the prayer with Joel, "Scott a baby!"

After a couple of weeks I said, "Scott, Joel's praying for you a baby!"

He went to Joel and said, "Joel, you stop that, we're too old to have a baby!"

BUT, IT WAS TOO LATE – SHE WAS ALREADY PREGNANT!!!!!!!

Joy of joys…wonder of wonder… a baby for the Froese family. Due Sept 9, 2006.

In July, Allen, Joel and I were almost out the door for church when the phone rang. I answered it and heard - "Well, we have a boy but he's awfully small!"

My legs wouldn't hold me up.. Allen came over and grabbed me and the phone. "He only weighs two and a half pounds! They had to take him last night because Sarah was in trouble. She had preëclampsia and her blood pressure was off the charts. They just ripped her open and grabbed him out. It was brutal!

We are at Zion Hospital, but don't come down today, we are just worn out!"

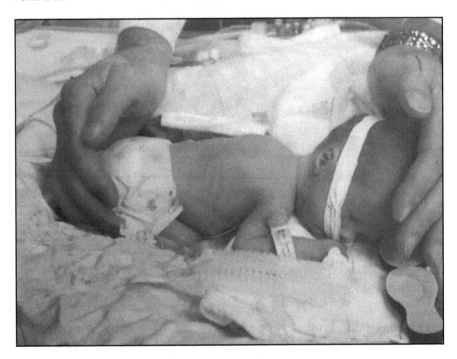

Kaden James Froese

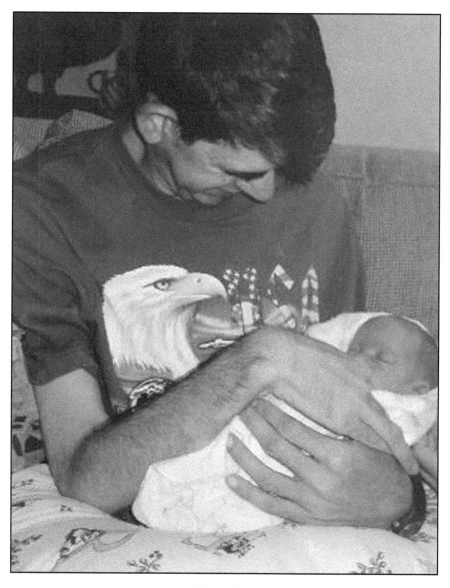

Uncle Joe

My Prayer Partner

During the years since I had retired, I was used to having the mornings alone as my time with God. I would spend hours in my Bible and study books. On the first day after we brought Joel home, I got up at 6:00a.m. and was very quiet so I wouldn't wake him. I made coffee and sat down – and here came Joel. Oh no! I prepared his coffee and he sat down with me, his Bible in his lap. The next day I got up an hour earlier – 5:00 a.m. Again, I was very quiet and again, here came Joel. I sent an SOS to God and I said, "Help Lord, what am I going to do here?" Instantly, I heard Him reply, "I thought you wanted a prayer partner!"

OH, OK! From that day forward, Joel and I got up at 6:00a.m., had our coffee and listened to a Jimmy Swaggart music CD and worshiped the Lord. We then opened our Bibles and had a wonderful time with God. For the next thirteen years Joel was my prayer partner.

The week after Joel moved home, at dinner one night, Allen, Joel and I talked about Joel's being baptized. He had asked Jesus to forgive his sins and live in his heart years before, but he'd never taken this next step.

"Joel, on Sunday you need to go up to the Pastor, at the invitation, and let him know you want to be baptized."

In a Baptist Church, at the close of the service, the Pastor gives an invitation to anyone in the congregation who may not have invited Jesus to be the Lord of their lives, to come forward for prayer. Also, anyone who wants to be baptized and join the church is invited to come up to the pastor as he stands, waiting.

Sure enough, at the end of the service that next Sunday, without my prompting, Joel got up out of his seat and went up to the pastor. I let him go alone but was on my way up to translate when I saw this look on the pastor's face that said, "Help! What is he saying?"

Everyone in the congregation got such a charge out seeing Joel baptized the following Sunday.

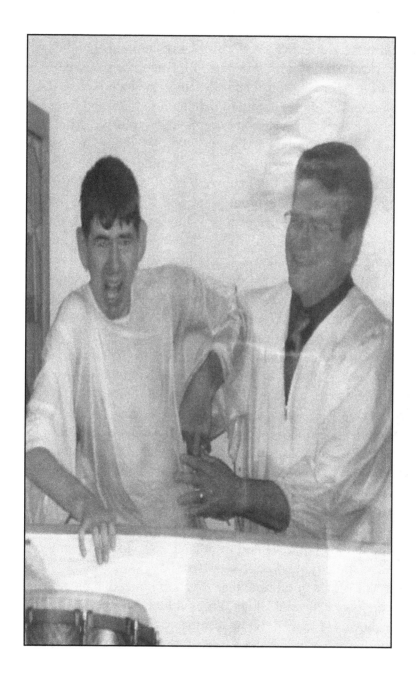

There were so many obstacles to overcome in making a place for Joel in his new environment. Lots of social workers later, Joel had a place with the United Cerebral Palsy workshop in Escondido.

He worked daily from 9:00 to 3:30. But since we lived in Vista, a neighboring town about fifteen miles away he had to have transportation. Thankfully, after a month of driving him back and forth we made contact with the LIFT program with the local transit district. This program was strictly for the handicapped people within the community.

So Joel left home about 7:30 each morning and returned after 4:00 in the afternoon. He was so happy. I was so happy. And even dad was so happy. Joel's presence in our home was a lot of work but so worth it. Never again would I have to take him back to San Diego, for another month that we wouldn't be together. His joy just spilled over onto everything. And, Allen had a sports partner. Joel loved baseball and football. They each had a remote to the same television and sometimes Joel would get so frustrated when his dad would change it on him- just for fun. He didn't speak much, but it didn't mean he wasn't vocal. He could holler with the best of them.

Allen was still working full time and more so he didn't care how much Joel and I traveled. I had been wanting to take a cruise but Allen wasn't interested so I thought I'd see how Joel would do. Our first cruise was only a three - night cruise to Ensenada, Mexico. We took dressy clothes and both enjoyed every part of it except for sharing a table. I was so conscious of other people paying their money for this experience and maybe they wouldn't like to have Joel's faltering eating. We had practiced at home on what utensils to use and he was on his absolute best behavior but after the first meal I thought best if we dined alone. The staff were good to let us know it wasn't necessary to leave the table...but I wanted to be able to relax and enjoy our meal and not be so uptight.

We had such a good time that we soon booked another – only this time there was a "formal" night. I rented Joel a tuxedo and fancy patent leather shoes. He looked SO handsome. When we got the photos back from the formal evening and I opened the envelope, my heart almost stopped. Joel looked absolutely normal and more handsome than I could ever have imagined. We were in the cocktail area awaiting dinner that evening when a lady came up to me and said, "Thank you for bringing your son. He looks wonderful!"

On our third cruise, again on the formal night Joel was again preening around, knowing how handsome he was when a woman came down the grand staircase, stared at him, and said. "Joel Froese?" Startled, I said, "Yes, he is Joel."

"I worked with him at the Home of Guiding Hands!" she was astounded at seeing him in this setting. "Oh my gosh, Joel, you are so handsome." He blushed and looked at his feet. "Joel, do you remember me?" "Es," he grinned.

I was as excited as she. "But that's been thirty - five years ago! How did you recognize him?"

"I would know him anywhere. He was one of my all -time favorites!"

You just never know when a blessing will rise up and smack you in the face. This woman was overcome with how wonderful he looked, all grown up and in a tuxedo on a cruise ship. And, I was stunned at how my son, my very limited, unspeaking son, had made such a lasting impression on this woman and blessed the lives of others on the boat. As the photographer poised us on the grand staircase, I noticed people looking up at us and smiling.

I believe it was on this same cruise when Joel and I were headed to the pool area several floors up from our room. We were just down the hallway from our room and I had to run back to the room for something I forgot and said, "Joel you stand right here and I'll be right back!" It took longer than I thought it would to locate the item but I finally found what I needed and rushed back to where he was supposed to be and he wasn't there. I ran to the nearest elevator. No Joel! "Oh, God!!! Where is Joel?" This ship is HUGE...with eight or so levels.... I ran up to the purser's desk.... "Excuse me, I've lost my handicapped son. Could you help me find him!" He put out an alert to the other staff and we all began a floor by floor search. I was almost in tears when I stumbled off the elevator on the Lido deck, where the pool is. There was my son - sitting in a deck chair - waiting for me. I almost screamed with relief! It was another of those maddening times when I was so proud that he showed ingenuity, yet, so overwrot with anxiety that I wanted to strangle him....

A Brother's Love

All throughout Joel's life, Scott tried to make it as fun for him as possible. Joel's well-being was always upper most in Scott's mind. He has such a creative mind and when he came up with a great present, it was also a precious gift for me.

We were celebrating one of Joel's birthdays at a local Chinese restaurant and Joel reached into a bag and pulled out a box of cereal. Allen and I looked at each other and then Joel began to squeal, "Me!! Look mom, ME! We looked at the box he was holding up. Sure enough, there was his picture on a Wheaties Box. That was SO AMAZING. Joel in his Special Olympics medals plastered the side of the box. All the Chinese wait staff huddled around the table exclaiming their delight.

When Joel and I moved into our new home, I contacted the Kellogg cereal company for permission to make a copy of that photo into a huge poster for his wall. This photo didn't really appear on the Wheaties boxes at the store. Scott photoshopped it.

At Joel's work, they always dressed up for Halloween. One year I asked Joe what he wanted to dress as and he said, "A baseball player!" He loved baseball and Football – was a great fan of the Padres and Chargers. Knowing how much he loved baseball I said, "Okay, buddy, you are going to be a ball player!

I went to a pro shop and got the works. His name on the back of a Detroit Tigers jersey. His dad donated his baseball glove and Joe looked so great his daddy took some wonderful pictures of him.

Come the next Christmas morning, Scott said, "Joel, your present is in the mailbox!" Joel hurried up to the mailbox and came back into the house yelling, "Me ... on the Sports Illustrated!" We looked, flabbergasted. Sure enough, on the cover of the Sports Illustrated was a photo of Joel in his baseball uniform. Headlines read, "Froese quits Padres to join the Detroit Tigers." There is a big long article in the magazine that tells his batting average...his family life...and how many millions he would be making with the Tigers. Plus, there were also baseball cards for him to hand out to his friends.

Allen

Allen Froese was a very unique man. He had a dry wit that could turn a serious conversation into a hilarious one with just one comment. He was stoic and very silent. His motto was: Poor planning on your part does not necessitate an emergency on mine. With that philosophy he could drive a person crazy! But, he was also a loveable teddy bear.

Allen didn't retire until he was seventy. He enjoyed his work and the people he worked with at Heller Ford. One of his friends, John Tessman commented, "I had breakfast with Allen for twenty-five years, and Allen had never once initiated a conversation."

When our family was blessed with Kaden, this became the high point of his life. He loved his family, but was overjoyed at our grandson. He and Kaden were an item. And Kaden had eyes for Papa only. From the time we brought Kaden home from the neo-natal unit at Zion Hospital, Allen and I kept Kaden at our home several days a week while his mom and dad worked.

He taught Kaden how to hammer, how to saw and how to dig holes as soon as he could walk. They spent hours in the garage "working." Work was one of Kaden's first words.

When they got tired they would go in and take a nap.

November 8th 2008, Allen and I celebrated our 50th wedding anniversary. Scott, Joel and Sarah gave us a wonderful party. Our first Christian friends, John & Marilee Todd and Amy and her husband came from Florida; Buddies, Barbara & Ralph Kelly from Texas and Doris Poole from Arkansas also were in attendance.

Three weeks later, we were preparing to accompany John and Marilee Todd, on a cruise to the Caribbean celebrate their 70th wedding anniversary, if you can imagine such a thing!

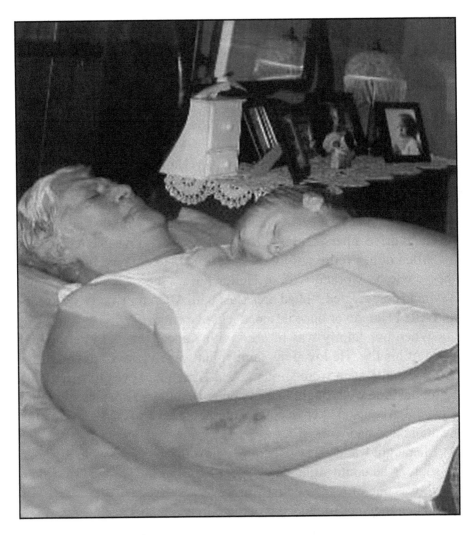

On Thursday of that week, we got a phone call from Allen's niece, "I just wanted to let you all know that my daddy lay down to take a nap today. When he didn't come out in a couple of hours, I went to see about him. He was gone!" Just like that! She told me that he had just been fitted for a C-Pap machine but hadn't used it when he took his nap. I went out to where Allen was reclining in his chair. "Honey, George just died!"

"What!"

"He lay down this afternoon to take a nap and didn't awaken." We were both stunned. How can something like that happen so fast!

That following Saturday, as usual, we had Kaden with us. As per our Saturday afternoon routine, we had lunch and I helped Joel lie down across his bed so he could watch tv until he fell asleep. I said to Allen, "Honey, you put the dishes in the sink and I'll give Kaden a bath. We'll meet you in bed." It wasn't more than ten minutes until we joined him. As always Kaden wanted to sleep on papa's chest, but today he was already asleep when we got in bed, "Kaden, let's be quiet so we don't awaken papa." So, he lay across my chest and we promptly fell asleep.

I awoke an hour later and went out into the living room and left them still both asleep. I was in the process of hanging the portrait I had made for Allen's 50th anniversary gift. BJ Simon, our next door neighbor is a portrait artist and does wonderful work. She used a photograph I snapped one day while the three of us were walking.

Allen had sat down on a stump and Kaden went up to him and they were talking with Kaden looking up to Allen. I knew the instant I saw the photo that this was an amazing picture. Allen had been thrilled I presented him with this treasure at our anniversary party.

Scott and Sarah both walked into the house to pick up Kaden. We put up the portrait and were admiring it.

I went in the bedroom to get Kaden up and as I did I noticed that Allen hadn't moved since he lay down. I started looking at his chest and I didn't see it moving. I hurried around the bed and touched his cheek. "Honey! HONEY!!" It was ice cold!

"Scott," I screamed. He came running into the bedroom. One glance and he began doing CPR on his dad and told me to call 9-1-1. In minutes the paramedics were there and they laid him out in the floor to work on him, but it was no use. He had died in the ten minutes it took for Kaden and me to get in bed.

Allen also had a C-Pap machine which he never used when he took a nap because Kaden was scared to see his papa in that contraption.

Friends and neighbors began to gather around us. Someone called our pastor and said, "Jerry, Allen is dead!"

Jerry replied, "He is not! I just talked with him this morning."

We were all in such shock! How does someone take the dishes off the table, put them in the sink, lie down and die in less than ten minutes.

When the paramedics finally quit working on him, I asked them to put Allen back in bed. He looked for all the world like he was still napping. I asked everyone to allow the family a few minutes alone. I called

Sarah and Joel into the bedroom where Scott, and I were. She crawled up beside him in the bed. We got Joel a chair to sit beside the bed. I asked him, "Honey, do you know what has happened?" "Es, Dad's in heaven!" Through our tears, what a precious time we had together in that bedroom, thanking God for all that Allen had been to us.

The day after Allen died, the other Froese's were coming over to our house and Kaden said, "Going to see Papa?"

Scott tenderly replied, "Kaden, Papa won't be there tonight. He has gone to live in Heaven."

Normally, when Kaden walked in our front door the first words out of his mouth were, "Where's Papa? Papa, Papa." And he would hunt him down. On this night he didn't once ask where Papa was. Never again did he ask for his Papa. How does a two-year old child understand, as he seemed to?

It was so ironic that on December 6th, 2008, the date we were to board our cruise in Florida, we had a celebration of Allen's life at our Lifeway Baptist Church.

Allen had died three days after his brother-in-law, in the very same way.

Always, when Allen and I would hit a milestone of marriage we'd say to each other, "Well, we made it!" Some times during the years, it was day by day… things can get really tough in marriage – BUT. The night we were approaching the restaurant to celebrate our 50th wedding anniversary we looked at each other and said,

"Well, we made it!" I think there was a verbal sigh in each of our minds - I think the 50th that is the golden ring every couple is reaching for.

But, at seeing him laying so peacefully on our bed this was.

For richer for poorer, in sickness and in health, til death do us part!"

We Made it!

Our New Lives

In the months ahead, Scott and I decided we would trade houses. Our family home where the boys grew up, was on a half-acre plot and Scott's house was two blocks from town and had only a little postage stamp yard. Sounded like a great trade to me. Allen had been such a wonderful provider for our family that we were able accomplish this.

While the transition was happening, Joel and I took a month-long car trip to visit friends and family in the southwest. Scott and Sarah remodeled their new home and when we returned from our trip I had our new home painted and polished and we moved in. Just Joel and me. That first night was very spooky. I had left my parent's home to marry. At 68, I was "home alone!"

During the months after Allen's death, Joel and I continued to attend Lifeway Baptist Church where we'd been members for 35 years. We loved the folk like family but I had become "spirit-filled" thirty years prior.

I had yearned for like-minded believers for years, but Allen was so comfortable in our church that I felt my place was beside him. One Sunday we were in the midst of Sunday worship when the Lord spoke to my heart,

"You don't have to stay here any longer!" As sad as I was to leave our church family, I knew I had heard from God, so Joel and I began visiting the different congregations within our city, finally choosing to affiliate with Vista Christian Fellowship, a Four-Square Church. How we both loved the lively services and the worship. They quickly absorbed us into the life of the church and I began working with the single women. (That was a shock to realize I was now a single woman.) Especially after being married fifty years.

Joel and I continued to travel, taking cruises and car trips. When his fiftieth birthday was approaching I said, "Joel what do you want for your birthday?" "Hawaii!" was his reply.

"You mean you want us to take a trip to Hawaii?"

"Yep!"

"Okay, buddy that's what we'll do!"

Before we knew it, we were landing on the Island of Kauai, the garden island. We rented a red convertible and checked in to our beautiful room right on the ocean. Joel grabbed the Gideon Bible and the remote control to the television and he was happy. I had a lovely patio where I could read and listen to the surf. We explored every part of the island with the top down. How fun!!!

One day, I went into Hilo Hattie's to do some shopping. Joel wanted to stay in the car. When I came out I couldn't see the car anywhere. I was almost in panic mode when I did a double take. Joel had put the top up on the convertible. I was amazed. When I jumped into the car he was so proud of himself that I didn't have the heart to yell at him.

When we travel, he is always in charge of the room key. One day it proved very fortuitous. We had lunch at an out of the way place about 20 miles from the hotel. When we arrived back, Joel handed me the room key and we unlocked the door and entered. As I was looking about me I realized I didn't have my purse. My heart sank. I must have left it at the restaurant. "Oh, Lord, you must help us!" We jumped into the car and hightailed it back to the restaurant, only to find that they were closed.

I went around the building looking everywhere for someone who might still be there, with no luck. There was a house next door. I had to bang repeatedly on the door to get someone's attention but finally a very nice, spaced out fellow answered the door and a cloud of marijuana fumes drifted into my face. When I told him my story he said, "No worries!!!

He gave me a phone number to call and said everything would be "cool!" Resigned to having to wait until the next day to contact the restaurant, we <u>slowly</u> drove back to the hotel...since I had no driver's license. Thankfully, when I called the restaurant the next morning they assured me they had my purse with our passports, and plane tickets ...and all our money, in it. Relief flooded my heart. Joel and I had prayed and put it all in God's hands but...I'm afraid I still had anxiety. Sometimes it's really scary to be the one in charge. Joel and I flew home after our Island vacation with light hearts and lots of memories.

We hadn't been at VCF very long when I ran into a woman who had been an acquaintance some ten years past. Since I'd last seen her she had been married briefly and had gone through a fire. She was burned over most of her body. Thankfully, her pretty face hadn't been touched. One ear had been burned off but she camouflaged it well with her blond hair. She was in her late fifties and was tall and willowy. She would sit behind me in church and it seemed like she was always weeping over the treatment she was getting from the people in whose home she rented a room. I tried to encourage her, but nothing seemed to help.

About this time I began to hear in my spirit, "Ask LaJuanna to live with you!"

"NO!!!"

It seemed like every Sunday I heard the exact same thing. "Ask LaJuanna to live with you!"

"NO, Lord...Joel and I are doing just fine!!! I've never been on my own before. I don't want to share my home!"

It didn't matter what excuse I gave the Lord, the next Sunday I would hear, "Ask LaJuanna to live with you! I was being leaned on big time! But I was adamant that I didn't want someone to live with us.

Early one morning, I was driving to the Senior Center where I was volunteering. As I drove down the street I heard a bump. I looked back through my rear view mirror and saw three young people, one of whom was holding her arm. I stopped the car and said, "Did I just hit you?"

"Your rear-view mirror hit my arm!"

What in the world! I had seen these young people as I was going down the street but didn't think they were anywhere near my car! One of the other of the three got on her cell phone and called 9-1-1. Before long we were surrounded with every type of emergency vehicle.

I was leaning on the rear of my car watching all of the action. A young patrolman came up to me and asked me what happened. After I explained he said, "I wouldn't worry too much about it. We all have a bad day once in a while." I then proceeded to tell him that my bad day started yesterday, "I had just finished visiting a friend at the hospital and I stopped to get gas. I was so distracted that I drove off with the gas hose still in my car."

"OH!"

He wrote something on a piece of paper and handed it to me. "You'll need to go the Traffic Commissioner's office tomorrow. (Don't EVER volunteer information to a police officer!!!)

The paramedics transported the girl to the emergency room and we all left the scene. The girl had given me her phone number so I called her later that day and she said she was okay. Her elbow was just a little sore. "They gave me a prescription at the hospital but I don't have the money to have it filled."

I assured her I would be right over to take her to get the prescription filled. I took her to my pharmacy and the pharmacist said, "This is only for aspirin...don't you have those at home?" She shook her head so he filled the prescription. She walked out ahead of me and the pharmacist said, "You watch out, this looks a little fishy to me." (Sure enough she really milked it with my insurance company and they wound up giving her something like $25,000.)

But that wasn't the end of my bad day. The next day, I had Joel with me and we went to San Diego to the Traffic Commissioner office. I was called into the commissioner's office who asked me some questions and I thought we had a really good interview. "Go out into the waiting room and someone will see you in a few minutes." I sat down with Joel and we waited. Finally, an officer of the court came out and said, "I'll take your driver's license."

"What...What on earth do you mean? I have my handicapped son here and he has a doctor's appointment!"

"Well, then tomorrow your license will no longer be valid!" I was stunned.

"Sputter....sputter!!! For how long?"

"Sixty days. You'll have to go through all the hoops to get a new license!"

I walked out of that office in utter shock! As I was driving back to Vista, I heard THAT voice…

"<u>NOW</u>, do you want LaJuanna to live with you?" When the Hound of Heaven speaks – listen! Because He can play **hardball**!

I called her and asked if she'd like to come and "drive miss Daisy?" She was there the next day.

Three months later I got my license back and LaJuanna went from my house to caring for a friend who had just spent a year in a hospital. She stayed with Lillian for two years, until she died. While she was gone I built a little bedroom for her in the backyard of my home. After Lillian died, she moved back and lived with Joel and me for five years.

She was such a wonderful help… that God knew I needed. She cared for Joel so that I could take a couple of trips…she loved gardening so that was her job around the house. We had some happy times together. It was fun to watch her grow and do things she never dreamed she could. Before long she was crocheting blankets, she found she was an artist and painted many beautiful works of art. She had a tremendous sense of style. She could purchase some of the neatest things from the Goodwill and put them together and have smashing outfits. Our friends would call on Lajuanna to accompany them to thrift stores to help them find bargains.

Mornings at our house were a wonderful routine. After Joel was dressed for work he would get out all our devotionals and turn them to the proper day; find the Scripture verses and lay out all the prayer guides. I prepared our protein breakfast drink and then LaJuanna and I would join him for our devotions.

At 8:00 Bob, the bus driver, would back the bus down our street, He had to back it because there was no-where for him to turn around.

He would bound down the driveway and knock at our door, always so happy and joyful…what a wonderful friend he was to all of us. We gave him a protein drink and he would help Joel up the hill. Joe always had his hands full with his lunch box and his Bible. Bob would try to get him to allow him to carry his Bible….but nothing doing! Joel's Bible was never out of his hand.

As always, Joel kept us all on track. One of our friends made beautiful boxes with rolled up Scriptures inside. Joel loved them and placed one at each of our places at the table at every meal. No one <u>ever</u> ate at our table without reading the Scriptures.

In February, Joel, LaJuanna and I welcomed Paul Ogbeleje into our home. This young man from Nigeria was a student at Palomar College and was desperate for assistance, so he lived with us for the two years he was in school.

Joel loved to watch game shows on television but at 9:00pm he would come out of the tv room to announce that Joyce Meyers was on. We all headed in to watch with him. Then he got up out of his chair, turned the TV off and announced to the house it was 10:00 and time for bed. He and I would go into our room and sit in the little couch in front of our fireplace. He would put his arm around me and I would scooch down to lay my head on his shoulder and I'd read our bedtime devotional.

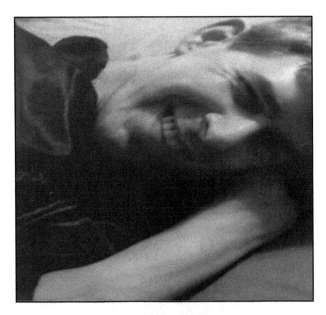

As his room was clear on the other side of the house, he just slept with me in my king-size bed as I never knew when he would have a seizure. I'd tuck him in on his side of the bed. We'd talk about heaven and how wonderful it would be when he got there and could do all the things he couldn't do now. He always loved that and his smile would light up his face. He would put his Bible under his pillow and, after positioning the angels around our house, at every door and window, we went to bed and slept so secure.

In February, shortly after Paul moved in to our house, he, LaJuanna and I were in the living room when I heard a slight noise coming from the room where Joel was. I ran in to find him on the floor in a major grand mal seizure. I knelt beside him and waited for the seizure to abate, then got him into bed.

He slept very soundly all that night and we awoke as usual the next morning. After I got him dressed and glanced up from making the bed. He was walking down the hallway and I couldn't see his head. I ran to him and looked him over good. I found he couldn't lift his head up. It was flopped all the way down on his neck. I called Bob to cancel his bus ride for the day and we hightailed it to the doctor. Dr. Mallo, our family doctor had an MRI done and it was inconclusive so he sent us to the hospital emergency room to have a CAT scan done.

We started at the doctor's office in the early a.m. and now, sitting in the emergency room it was almost ten o'clock at night. At some point during that long day, someone had given Joel a neck brace and he was a bit more comfortable. An emergency room is like the anti-room to hell, sitting for hours in the room filled with sick people of every sort.

That day began a long siege of pain for Joel and me. Dr. Mallo told us the tests were inconclusive and only showed that Joel had a bad sprain on his neck but other than pain pills could give us no answer. I began taking Joel to our family chiropractor several times a week. All Dr. Dan could do was rub his neck and back area with a low energy electric wand. We were all so grieved at watching him suffer.

By May we had to retire Joel from his sheltered workshop job. He always loved going to work and it broke my heart that he had to leave it, but it was just too long of a day to sit in a straight chair from 9:00 to

3:30. So we had a "retirement party" with cake, gifts and lots of slaps on the back for a job well done. He had worked there thirteen years.

Joel has severe scoliosis and for thirty years the Harrington rods supported his spine. The spine had begun to curve around the rods and on a good day Joel's back hurt, but now I could hardly bear what he was suffering. I just began crying out to God to please take him home to heaven. I enlisted all my friends to pray with me about this. I wept from a broken heart to see my beloved hurting so.

Finally, in August, after several additional visits to Dr. Mallo, he said he'd been talking to a friend of his about Joel. He strongly suggested we see Dr. Nguyen, a neurosurgeon. "Maybe he will be able to offer us some insight." He was as troubled as I over this difficulty Joel was in.

We were so hopeful but apprehensive in approaching this new doctor. We were sitting in the consultation room awaiting Dr. Nguyen when he bounded through the door. The first words out of his mouth were loud and exasperated!

"HE HAS A BROKEN NECK!!!"

By this time, we had a more sophisticated neck brace on Joel but he said, "That thing is on him all wrong." All of this before he even said hello. He took the time to gently reapply the brace correctly, showing me how it was to be done. "This is very critical. One slip of that neck in the wrong way and he would be paralyzed. I don't know how he has made it this long!"

He immediately began scheduling for surgery and that was that! Within a week we had a date of August 29.

As this was almost a month away, I scheduled a little vacation for the two of us. Joel loved to stay in

"Tells." I remember one trip we had been on for a couple f weeks. When Joel began to recognize landmarks along the road, he began to let me know he wasn't ready to go home and wanted to stay at a 'tell one more time…so 35 miles from home I pulled into a motel parking lot and we spent one more night on the road.

For this vacation we checked into the Bahia' Hotel in San Diego. By this time Joel had begun to wear his pain in a perpetual frown. His neck and back were so heartbreakingly crooked. I could hardly bare it.

Through this whole ordeal he had never complained. Never said ouch... never cried but I felt every moment of his agony. His only sign of pain was he ground his teeth.

A vacation for Joel is a new TV to watch. We got situated in a lovely suite and he searched the cabinets until he found the Gideon Bible. With his Bible and the TV remote he was a happy camper. I could go outside to read, or walk about the property. It was a very relaxing time for both of us. I managed to get him out of the room one afternoon to take some photos. After a few days it was time to go home and prepare for the surgery. "Please Dear Lord, do something for my beloved son!!!"

Joel and I got to the hospital about 6:30 am and our pastor was already there. We are so blessed to be a part of a loving fellowship and our pastor, Roger Friend, is an amazing man of God. He never misses a surgery. The night before, I had sensed the Lord wanted me to pray a special prayer for the surgeon before surgery.

That morning when Dr. Nguyen came in, I said, "Doctor, may we pray for you?" "Of Course!" was his reply. We all joined hands and I prayed, "Father – last evening You quickened my heart to what You wanted said to this man today, You told me to say 'God is the one who gives life and God is the one who takes it away' This isn't on you! blessed be the name of the Lord." Joel was alert and gave us all one of his amazing smiles. He was SO happy to finally be in a hospital. (He had wanted to go to a hospital for years!) I kissed him and they were off. My heart was stayed on Jesus that morning and my pastor was a comfort.

Really more quickly than I anticipated, Dr. Nguyen came out, pulling off his mask. "Well, Joel did really well! I fused his neck to where he will be able to look straight ahead. He won't have much play in the neck but he won't be in any pain!" My heart rejoiced!!!

After several hours in recovery Joe was finally wheeled into his room. Rather, I should say, our room because there was no way I was leaving him. This new state of the art hospital was all private rooms with a couch that made into a bed at night. It also had room service, so I could get meals brought up for me. Almost too good to be true! Joel had tubes protruding from his body, his neck was packed and braced but he groggily said, "Hi, Mom!" as I slipped his Bible under his hand.

In the last couple of days before we went to the hospital, I had made large signs, "Happiness is knowing Jesus, and several other things and Joel and I took our lawn chairs to a busy street corner, where we sat and held our signs. So, I decided to take that particular sign to the hospital and position it prominently in his room. We also had a beautiful box of Scriptures for our visitors. I brought our little boom box and every night we played our Christian music and we sang.

On Thursday afternoon, Joel's CNA came into the room and said, "Mary, what's in that little box?"

"Mai, that is one of Joel's ministries. He loves to give out those Scriptures. Open the box and take one." She opened the box and took out one of the rolled pieces of paper. She went over to the couch and sat down and read it aloud. "Mary, what does this mean?" I told her to the best of my ability what it meant and she replied, "Mary – I love God!" She was either Filipino or Vietnamese decent so I didn't know how much she know of God so I replied, " Oh, Mia I'm so glad. Have you asked Jesus to come into your heart to be your Savior."

"How do I do that!" By this time I'm jumping on the inside. I led her in a prayer inviting Jesus to come into her heart, to be her Savior and Lord. Then I said, "Mai. Do you see that man over in that bed. He is a Disciple of the Lord Jesus Christ. I believe with all my heart that God spoke to him back in February and said, "Joel, I have an assignment for you. It's going to be hard, but I need to use you so that Mai can come to know me!"

"Mai, THAT is how much God loves you!!!" About that time Pastor Roger came through the door and we all rejoiced that Mai had trusted Jesus to be her Savior!!! Joel was still very groggy so I went over and told him what had just happened. He smiled and fingered his Bible that lay beside him.

The next morning Dr. Nguyen came in to talk with Joel. "Hi, Joel. How are you doing, buddy?"

Joel smiled at him. The doctor then said, "Joel, today we are going to transfer you to rehab. You will stay there until you can walk and use your neck. Then you can go home. Okay!"

"NO!!" Joel replied loud and clear. He didn't want to leave the hospital.

I tried to intervene, "Oh, honey! Look, I bought you a new Charger lounge set to wear to rehab. You will really like it!"

"NO!!"

"Joel, we have to do this! I responded. "I'm going to leave for a couple of hours to take Paul to take his driving test. I'll be back this afternoon so we can move!" I told Mai what I was doing and she said, "While you're gone I'll give Joel a bath and get him dressed in his new Charger clothes."

I met Paul at the DMV and I threatened him, "Paul, if you don't pass this driving test THIS time, I'm gonna kill you!" (We'd already been through this twice.) A few minutes later he walked back to me beaming…. He had passed! SO, I took him to lunch to celebrate.

We had just ordered our lunch when the phone rang. It was rehab letting me know they were ready for Joel. Then a minute or so later I get another call. It is Dr. Nguyen. "Mary, where are you?"

"Oh, hi Doctor, I had some business to take care of."

"Mary, Joel's heart stopped.!" I turned to stone!

"What!"

"Mary, Joel is dead!" By now I am hyperventilating but I remember something. "Doctor, do you remember the prayer I prayed over you the day of Joel's surgery. "God gives life and He takes it away. This isn't on you!"

I grab hold of Paul and we fly out of the restaurant. I can still hardly breathe as He drives and I call Scott. "Scott, get to the hospital, now!" I call Lizzy, the friend who had been praying with me that Joel wouldn't have to suffer any more. When I tell her she screams, "Thank you Jesus!!!" and I call LaJuanna; I tell each of them to meet us at the hospital. Paul pulls up to the curb at the hospital and I jump out and fly to the elevator. It takes an eternity for that elevator to go to the 7th floor. I exit the elevator in a dead run and fly into his room.

I screech to a stop and look at my BELOVED SON. He lies in that bed with the most beautiful smile on his face. All the pain lines are gone. He is SO beautiful! I fall across his bed and my heart bursts into rejoicing and grief. Our God had spoken, "**Joel, your work here is done. Why don't you just go home with Me.**"

His nurse, Cheryl, hurried into the room when she saw me come in and through my tears I said, "What happened?"

"I was down the hall and I saw in my monitor that Joel's breathing was slowing down. I ran back, but when I got here he had quit breathing. He was gone! I called Code Blue but then remembered we had an advance directive for Joel."

I weep for a bit and then she says, "Mary I have to tell you, we on this floor will never be the same. We have seen how you cherished your son. I heard you all singing last night and how you prayed together. Thank you!"

As I looked at my beautiful son, I was immediately taken back to when my husband lay dead on his bed. He also had such a beautiful look of peace. At that moment, I knew that was exactly what happened to his daddy. Allen just stopped breathing. No pain, no heart attack! He just went home.

By this time, Paul has parked the car and rushed into the room and saw his friend.

Scott got there just a couple of seconds later. He began to weep and sat by Joel's side, caressing him. His long journey to connect with the brother he loved so much was finally completed.

Lizzy and LaJuanna rushed into the room and we all wept, laughed and praised God for His goodness in taking Joel home with Him.

Until that moment, I hadn't realized that if Joel's neck was fixed rigid so he could look straight ahead, he wouldn't be able to look down to feed himself. He couldn't look down to put his shoes on. Or play games on his IPad and a dozen other things, But now it was an -

Oh! Never Mind…He just went HOME!!!! Where he can see his Savior … Where he can READ his Bible! Where he can dress himself! Where he can talk up a storm and be understood! Where he can run and not get tired! Where he can play baseball!… Where he can reason with the prophets! I went into Scott's arms and we wept.

Epilogue

A week or so before Joel went into the hospital, I was sitting somewhere and I began to see a scenario play before me in my mind.

I saw Joel walking down a road with Jesus. Jesus was pointing out the sights of heaven. They came near a building and Jesus said, "Joel see that door over there. There are some guys waiting for you."

Joel walked through that door into a big league baseball locker room. The guys were all suited up and they yelled, "Hey, Froese We've been waiting for you – get dressed, we have a game to play." These guys, Joel recognized as big league players while here on earth. His cousin Charlie, who had been a Detroit Tiger, was among them!!! Joel looked down and there was a uniform with his name on the back. He quickly dressed and someone tossed him a ball and someone else threw him a mitt and said, "You're pitching!"

They all ran out of the locker room onto the field of a gigantic baseball arena. All the people of heaven were seated in the stands. As Joel looked around through the crowd, there was his daddy and his grandparents and there sat Jesus.

Then it was like a shade was pulled down in front of me and the vision was done. I think I told Joel what I saw but I told no one else. I just held it close to my heart.

On the Saturday of Joel's Homegoing Celebration, As I was leaving the house, the doorbell rang. I answered the door and it was the florist who had been to our home so many times that week. This time it was a bouquet of red long-stemmed roses. I sat it on the counter and read the card:

Dear Mom:

Thank you for not hiding me away, but immersing me Completely in life and letting me achieve my full potential.

I know it wasn't always easy, But I had a ball. Can't wait to see you again.

Love, Joe

(Scott sent this)

Scott and I stood on the veranda of the church and greeted all our old friends as they came to celebrate with us. Oh, what a joy to see people we hadn't seen in so long. The church was full of people whom Joel had blessed.

The celebration began with Joel's favorite song.

<u>*ON YOUR FIRST DAY IN HEAVEN*</u>

We'll it's a great, great morning, Your first day in aven
When you're strolling down the golden avenue.
There are mansions left and right, and
You'll thrill to every sight and the saints
Are always smiling saying, "How do you do!"
Oh, it's a great. Great morning, your first day in heaven
When you realize you're worrying days are through.
You'll be glad you were not idle, took time to read the
Bible It's a Great Morning for YOU!"

A SPECIAL PILGRIM'S PROGRESS
To the celestial City

The following day at church, I got up to go to the bathroom and as I walked up the aisle, Terry Heitger, stood up and took my arm. I looked over at him. He was weeping and shaking. He said, "Mary, this morning I had a vision of Joel!"

My heart began to pump, "Well, come outside so I can hear it! I exclaimed. We hurried out the foyer of the church.

I was puzzled because I didn't know this man. He was a pillar of the church but he normally sat on the far side of the sanctuary and I'd never had a conversation with him, except to say hi. He didn't know me, he didn't know Joel. He hadn't been to the celebration but now he was standing before me trembling and weeping.

"Mary, this morning I saw Joel in a gigantic baseball arena. <u>He had hit a home run and he was running the bases</u>, with his arms in the air praising God!"

I almost hit the floor!

Then I told him my part of the vision. We hugged and laughed and wept together. As we re-entered the sanctuary, Pastor Roger was talking about last night's celebration. I just continued on down the aisle and said, **"Pastor, you're not going to BELIEVE THIS!"**

Dr. Nguyen

For a year after Joel's home going, every time I'd turn on my I Phone the first thing I would see was Dr. Nguyen name and phone number. It showed up <u>every time</u> I opened my phone.

There was always a niggle in my spirit that I didn't have closure with him.

That day at the restaurant when he called with the sad news about Joel. I had gone outside so that I could hear him better when I heard him say, "Mary, Joel's dead!" He continued to talk... as I grabbed Paul and we rushed down the stairs, I could hear he was talking. He talked almost until we got into the car and I never knew what he was saying. In fact, that is the last time I spoke with him.

All this year, it was so strange that his name would show up on my phone. Finally, one day, I took the time to call his office. "I identified myself and asked if Dr. Nguyen would take a phone call from me, about his former patient?" His nurse said she would check and get back to me. A couple of days later she called and set up an appointment for a phone call. I was in the car when his office called to say he was on the line. I pulled over, shaking like a leaf!

"Dr., you may not even remember me. I'm Joel Froese's mother!"

He said, "Mary, of course I remember you and Joel!

It had occurred to me that he might think I was calling to say WHY DIDN'T YOU DO THIS OR THAT FOR MY SON, so I tried to put him at ease immediately. "Dr., this entire year I have wondered what you were saying to me after you told me Joel had died...I was running for the car and never got to talk with you again."

We had the most wonderful conversation for ten minutes or so as he told me how he had wanted to give Joel a few more good years by repairing his neck. I replied, "Oh, doctor!!! He is having a whole eternity of good years now. He is at home with his Savior. And I told him the story of the Heavenly Ballgame.

"Dr., I am so grateful for all you did for Joel and the beautiful floral arrangement you sent to us. My prayer for you is that before you leave this earth you give your heart to Jesus, the

One who loves you and gave you your gifting as a surgeon."

"Mary, I thank you so much for this call and to my dying day, I promise you

I'll never forget Joel Froese!"

Other Books by Mary Francess Froese

Heroes of a Special Kind
Mary Magdalene – From Pain to Promise
Working in God's Harvest, the Ken Steiner Story
The Country Pastor, The Charles Grasty Story

Mary Froese lives in Vista, California and would love to visit with you.
(760)419-8297
Joelsmother1960@gmail.com

CPSIA information can be obtained
at www.ICGtesting.com
Printed in the USA
FSHW012351070619
58766FS

9 781949 231670